Praise for *Vetting—The Making of a Veterinarian*

Vetting is more than a story; it's an allegory of life, using Dr. Freyburger's relationships with animals to transport us to the hidden crannies and fissures of our soul. A worthy read.

DONALD F. SMITH, DVM, Dean Emeritus,
Cornell University College of Veterinary Medicine

The lessons of life choices are hidden within the covers of Vetting. *Dr. Pete Freyburger shows us how he tried, failed, succeeded, and triumphed while serving his community, his family, his friends, and animals. The humor and passion that Pete shows as he learns about life and how his choices will frame his future can help all of us to lead the life we want.*

BARBARA CARR, Executive Director, SPCA Serving Erie County

This story is more than a personal account of Pete's life experiences and loving work with animals. Anyone who reads this book will truly know the caring man who has devoted his life to his family and his interesting patients. And, just as important, the reader will come to understand the challenges, joys, sorrow, excitement, and rewards experienced by all who dedicate their heart and soul to the wonderful profession of veterinary medicine.

JOSEPH E. SAVARESE, DVM, Professor and Chair,
Veterinary Technology Department, Medaille College, Buffalo, New York

Being a transplant to the Buffalo area, I read each chapter eager to learn more about the lives that my friends and colleagues led many years ago. Pete's down-to-earth writing style takes readers into the exam room, the treatment area, and the surgery settings of a veterinary hospital. It gives us an understanding of the stresses, joys, and triumphs of practicing veterinary medicine.

TIMM OTTERSON, DVM, Summer Street Cat Clinic
President, Pet Emergency Fund

VETTING

The Making of a Veterinarian

VETTING

vet'-ting – verb
1) to examine or treat an animal
2) to subject somebody or something to careful examination or scrutiny—especially when this involves determining suitability for something
3) to practice as a veterinarian

The Making of a Veterinarian

Commencement Day, May 28, 1976, Cornell University, Ithaca, NY
Photo of Original Graduation Cake Designed by Barbara Freyburger

Dr. Pete Freyburger

PJF PUBLICATIONS
TONAWANDA, NY

VETTING: The Making of a Veterinarian

Copyright © 2009 by Peter J. Freyburger, DVM

ISBN: 978-0-9824503-4-5
Library of Congress Control Number: 2009927911

Some individual names may have been changed to protect the privacy of individuals. The chronological order of some events may have been altered.

Printed in the United States of America

Published by PJF Publications—North Tonawanda, New York
For more information visit **www.pjfpub.com**

Dedicated to Barbara
She made the journey possible.
She walked each road beside me.
She heard it all before.

FOREWORDS

Greek mythology tells us that the goddess Athena sprang fully formed from the head of Zeus. Rather than such a sudden and dramatic occurrence, for mere mortals, we become who we are via a journey through time filled with smaller, far less sensational, yet still fascinating events. In this captivating autobiographical account, we take this journey with Peter as he traces the route he followed as a young man to become a successful and respected Doctor of Veterinary Medicine.

In this collection of tales, Peter tells us about his blossoming romance with future bride Barbara, the births of his three sons, the challenges of vet school, his crisis of professional confidence, the trials of his early years in practice, the sometimes eccentric people he worked with and learned from, and of course his unforgettable patients and their equally memorable owners. The stories vary in character. Some of them are heartwarming; some are sad. Others are humorous, educational, or inspiring. All of them are interesting and enjoyable.

At sometime in his or her life, almost every young pet owner imagines a career as a veterinarian. Very, very few ever get to achieve that dream. Through Dr. Freyburger's experiences, we have a chance to know the joys and the sorrows of small animal medicine.

I had the privilege to see the early drafts of *VETTING: The Making of a Veterinarian.* The first chapter I read was the story of Susie the beagle, and I was an instant fan. I couldn't wait for Peter to e-mail the next chapter to me.

Peter and I were classmates and friends in junior and senior high school, where we shared a common interest in nature and love of the outdoors. After graduating, we traveled our separate paths. His led to the Brighton-Eggert Animal Clinic, just a few minutes' walk from the house where he grew up. Mine led me half a world away to Japan, where my daughter is now enrolled in veterinary school. Last year, she had the opportunity to spend some time with Dr. Freyburger at his clinic, leaving her with a lasting impression of what a veterinarian should be.

ALAN BERGMAN
Kenmore East Senior High School—
Class of 1969
Instructor at Hosei University—
Tokyo, Japan

Vetting is a book that brings together the elements of the life of a small-town veterinarian. Strong family ties, love of animals, educational drive, hard work, vision, ethics, and romance are all part of Dr. Pete Freyburger's fulfilling life.

As each chapter is read, the reader is provided a rare opportunity to vicariously live the life of another. This work is so personal that the reader is swept away, wishing that Pete were not just the author, but a personal friend.

The lessons of life choices are hidden within the covers of this book. The struggle to make good choices and then follow through is universal to humankind. Pete shows us how he tried, failed, succeeded, and triumphed while serving his community, his family, his friends and animals.

The connection Pete makes between himself and the animals he treats, the bond between the pet and owner, and the relationship between pet owners and veterinarians intertwines through the pages of this book, leading us on a journey of discovery. We witness the struggle of a young man breaking into his career while building relationships with contrary pet owners, a redheaded beauty, established veterinarians, and hundreds of animal patients. We read on to discover how Pete's family and practice grew and how each achievement and accomplishment was matched by new opportunities and interesting predicaments. Following this path of life is a special opportunity for each of us as we must face our own challenges. The humor and passion that Pete shows as he learns about life and how his choices will frame his future can help all of us to lead the life we want.

I have known Dr. Freyburger for fifteen years. As the director of the local SPCA, I always knew I respected Pete. Reading his book explains to me the making of this man and why I was always drawn to his down-to-earth approach to the veterinary profession. Little did I know that this man was also a fine storyteller, one with a fine story to tell.

BARBARA CARR
Executive Director
SPCA Serving Erie County

I have known Dr. Pete Freyburger for thirty years or so. Our relationship started out on a professional level. But soon we found ourselves traveling together in a group with other veterinary couples on trips that combined continuing education with new destinations. Those travels allowed us to forge a friendship at a different level.

Unlike Pete, I ultimately decided to go to Iowa State University for my veterinary training. I knew when I started that I wanted to work on large animals. In particular I wanted to work on horses and range cattle. As a growing child, I had watched Gene Autry, Roy Rogers, the Lone Ranger, and the Cisco Kid. I thought the greatest thing ever would be to grow up to be a cowboy. I grew up on some acreage in Western New York, where we had horses, beef cattle, pigs, chickens, sheep, and an assortment of pets. It was a great time in my life. I had two brothers and a sister. Mom and Dad always encouraged us to do the right thing and be really good at whatever path we chose to follow. Eventually, when I was in high school, I had to fill out a questionnaire for the guidance counselor about what career I wanted to pursue. That was the first moment I can remember wanting to be a veterinarian. I had to ask the teacher how to spell it. After that, of course, the decisions became easier.

My college years were also a good time in life. I learned so much, not only about animals, but about people. We started treating animals in our last two years of veterinary school. I never knew how hard horses and cows could kick until I started to work on range animals. After a year and several injuries, a lightbulb went on, and I thought about smaller animals, namely dogs and cats. I loved it.

After a stint in the Army, I knew that it was small animal practice for me and that I wanted to stay in Western New York. How nice it was to meet all of the veterinarians in the area, including Pete Freyburger. He was younger, but we both had the same ideas and goals.

As the years went on, we saw each other frequently, and of course our friendship grew. I looked forward to our time together on our trips. Eventually, with any group of veterinarians, the conversation gets around to pets, clients, and cases. Pete could always remember better stories than I could. And now he has written some of those for all to enjoy and shared his personal journey with you. Ah, even better!

JOHN C. LAURIE, DVM
Retired Former Owner
Orchard Park Veterinary
Medical Center

As a young veterinarian who practices in the Buffalo, New York, area, I have been fortunate to follow in the footsteps of Dr. Pete Freyburger and all of his contemporaries. Being a transplant to the Buffalo area, I read each chapter, eager to learn more about the lives that my friends and colleagues led many years ago. Pete's down-to-earth writing style takes readers into the exam room, the treatment area, and the surgery settings of a veterinary hospital. It gives us an understanding of the stresses, joys, and triumphs of practicing veterinary medicine.

I especially enjoyed Pete's depiction of his relationship with and his reliance on the dedicated staff with which he has been blessed to work side by side over the years. His autobiography captures the many ways pets enrich our lives and how owners, veterinary technicians, veterinarians, and even veterinarian's families work and make sacrifices for the well-being of our four-legged friends.

Pete's story leads us through his idealistic youth, his academic years, the growth of his family, his early disillusionment and burnout with the stresses and challenges of daily practice, and finally his realization that it is so very worthwhile after all.

As the president of the Pet Emergency Fund, an animal charity founded by the Niagara Frontier Veterinary Medical Society, this book reminded me why so many talented veterinarians and technicians dedicate their lives to our profession. Dr. Freyburger has been an active member in that society for over thirty years, and his clinic has been a strong proponent of the Pet Emergency Fund since its inception. On behalf of the board of the fund, we are pleased and honored that Pete has chosen to support our efforts by selecting our efforts as one the pet-related charities to be supported via this book.

TIMM OTTERSON, DVM
Summer Street Cat Clinic
President, Pet Emergency Fund

Contents

The 1970's

I DID NOT WRITE THESE STORIES. I put the words on paper. The stories wrote themselves. Veterinarians are fortunate people. We work with some of people's most precious possessions—their pets. We also work with pet owners at their most vulnerable moments, when they let their guard down and when they are experiencing some of the rawest of emotions created by the human-animal bond. These experiences lead to some incredible stories that are sometimes stranger than fiction. Most any veterinarian could pen a few of these stories from their real-life experience.

But first, a bit of history may be helpful to put it all in perspective. During the 1970s, there were only eighteen veterinary schools in the United States. Then, as now, one often heard it said that gaining admission to a veterinary college was more difficult than gaining admission to a medical college. At the same time, a change was taking place in households everywhere in regard to pet ownership. Pets, rapidly becoming more important in many people's lives, began to be celebrated as true family members rather than mere possessions. Pet owners gradually demanded better and better medical care for their four-legged family members. Veterinary schools were finding it important to prepare more doctors for small animal care and fewer for large animal medicine.

Many things helped to contribute to the rise in status of pets in our society. Not insignificant during these changing years were the writings of Dr. James Wight, from England. Known better by his pen name, James Herriott, his series of wonderful books began with *All Creatures Great and Small*, which first gained recognition in 1973, one year after I began my studies in veterinary school. Herriot's writings were in the right place at the right time and helped to elevate both the status of animals in our society as well as the perceptions of and respect for veterinary medicine as a profession. His writing quickly became the inspiration for those who aspired to become veterinarians in the years that followed.

A different book, however, influenced me. As an assignment in freshman English, I had to pick a book from *The New York Times* bestseller list to read. I chose to read *The Making of a Surgeon*, by William Nolen, MD. The wonderful stories in those pages described his internship and residency at Bellevue Hospital in Manhattan. That reading ignited in me a desire to combine my interest in medicine with my passion for dealing with animals.

During my first years in the profession, I met and worked with many fascinating pets and their owners. Those animals and their caregivers, along with my co-workers and people in my personal life, molded and made me who I am today, and this book tells that story. It describes my journey into veterinary medicine along with my journey through the years with Barbara, my wife.

Many of the stories in this book are now more than three decades old. Some names long since forgotten had to be recreated. Other names were changed to protect the privacy of the individuals described. Some names, especially those of the veterinary technicians, are real. Many fascinating stories, all based on real events, create the backbone of the journey described in this book.

CHAPTER 1
First Solo Weekend
West Seneca, June 1976

THE FIRST HOUR FLOWED BY SMOOTHLY. People who make early morning appointments on Saturday generally have other plans for the day. They are anxious to get in and out without delay. Only small talk was necessary. At 9:15, Paula, a veterinary technician, appeared with an ashen look on her face. Paula was a registered nurse who had abandoned the ranks of human medicine to work with pets.

"We have a hit-by-car coming right over. Sounds bad," whispered Paula.

"OK," I responded, pretending to be calm. "Keep Exam Two open, and set up for an IV in the treatment room. Let me know as soon as it arrives."

My thoughts were spinning out of control during the next office call; the possible scenarios were endless. Thankfully, the cat in this room only needed suture removal. Even I could handle that while distracted.

After a mere five days on the job as a licensed veterinarian, it was my turn to handle a weekend alone. That meant seeing patients on Saturday morning and dealing with any emergencies for the balance of the weekend. In this suburban practice south of Buffalo, New York, two appointments were booked every fifteen minutes on Saturday morning, twice the normal pace. The appointment schedule was always full on Saturday despite dismal economic times. Recently, both Bethlehem Steel and Republic Steel had shut their doors and were in the process of mothballing plants that were located a few short miles from our clinic. Many thousands of blue-collar workers had been laid off, and the closing of these once enormous plants devastated

3

everyone. Our communities were becoming the regions that helped coin a new national term—the Rust Belt.

As a recent graduate, the idea of tackling Saturday morning appointments alone was formidable. A license to practice medicine is in a way similar to a license to drive a car. Every new driver is qualified to drive. However, as each stop sign or bend in the road approaches, new drivers still have to think about when to accelerate, when to reach for the brake, and how to steer through a turn. Practicing medicine is no different. The new graduate has to think about what questions to ask, what diseases to consider, what medications to use, and at what dosage. The new veterinarian reaches for reference material to double-check even the simplest decisions. On top of that, one is expected to chat politely with the owner and pet the patient, even though most of the doctor's brain is lost in some medical jungle. In six months time, most of these things would become instinctive, just as the experienced driver is comfortable behind the wheel. Yet here I was, on my own for the first time and not feeling comfortable about it at all.

The appointment book revealed that there would be thirty-two pets to examine by noon. My personal approach to stressful situations has always been to create strange ways to track progress, especially when the road ahead appears hopeless. On a desk between the two exam rooms, I placed a scratch pad with the number 32 scribbled near the top. After each office call, I would cross that number out and write down the next lower one. This approach to stress was a silly idiosyncrasy, but it worked for me. By reminding myself of bits of progress or accomplishment, the task ahead seemed more reachable.

Before the next pet was settled into Exam 1, the commotion down the hall told me that my first solo trauma case had just arrived. On the table in Exam 2, a petite young beagle named Susie lay almost lifeless on a makeshift plywood stretcher. Rapid, shallow breathing and pink foam at the corner of her mouth confirmed my worst fears. The owner was sobbing, trying to say something, but all my peripheral vision noted was a tall, heavyset fellow with dark hair. My stethoscope revealed a faint but racing heartbeat. The dog's mouth was open revealing ghost white gums. There was little question that Susie was hemorrhaging internally and deep in shock.

I felt tears collect in the corners of my eyes. Fate had dealt a wicked blow. My family had raised and bred beagles during my high school years, and all I could see on the table was one of our six-month-old pups from years earlier. My first unsuccessful treatment would hurt all the more.

"Take her straight to treatment and start an IV," I said, hoping that my voice was more a bark than a whimper. Paula and another assistant carried the stretcher out of the room and raced toward the back of the hospital.

"Susie is bleeding badly internally, and she may not make it," I said to Mr. Pascal, the owner, as I started toward the door, avoiding eye contact. "We need to give her fluids and shock medication as rapidly as possible to try to bring her blood pressure up. I'll have a technician monitor her constantly and check on her myself between each appointment. We'll do all we can, and I'll call you at home as soon as her condition changes in either direction."

Mr. Pascal was trying to mumble between sobs about the accident as he headed out the other door.

Paula already had a catheter in a vein and was hooking up the IV when I arrived in the treatment room. I injected a vial of fast-acting cortisone to try to counteract the shock, and then I headed for the next office call, leaving Paula on vigil. Between each exam, I scooted back to the treatment area to check on Susie's progress. Unfortunately, the heartbeat became steadily fainter, slower, and shallower. I had no access to whole-blood transfusion equipment, and emergency surgery was simply not feasible in most veterinary settings in 1976. Unfortunately, my embryonic clinical judgment was correct. Susie passed away within thirty minutes of arrival.

Susie had arrived as the number 22 appeared on the scratch pad monitoring my progress. Before the number 19 appeared, she was gone. I knew it was time to pick up the phone and call Mr. Pascal to deliver the bad news. It was time for me to experience the pain of that call for the first time. After avoiding the inevitable through two more exams, I could procrastinate no longer. As I picked up the phone, my heart seemed to race faster than Susie's had only an hour earlier.

"Mr. Pascal, I'm really sorry, but Susie didn't make it. The internal damage was just too great to reverse. She never regained consciousness and passed on

5

a few minutes ago. All I can assure you is that she probably felt little pain and never knew what happened."

"This is all my fault Doc," Mr. Pascal said between sobs. "I was working in the yard, and apparently the gate didn't latch behind me. We live on a four-lane highway. She never had a chance. I didn't know she was out of the yard until the brakes squealed. I have no one to blame but myself."

I had no idea how to respond, but somehow managed to respond with a cracking voice.

"Accidents happen, Mr. Pascal. Don't be too hard on yourself. It's very obvious that you deeply loved her. I'm certain she knew that." I paused as long as possible before continuing. "I know this is a terrible time to ask this question, but since we close at noon, I have to ask now. Do you want us to take care of Susie's body? She would be buried on a nearby farm unless you have other preferences."

"No," he responded with a sniffle. "Our family owns property south of the city. She loved it down there. All I can do for her now is bury her there myself."

"That's fine if you feel up to it," I said. "Will you be able to pick up her body this morning?"

"No. I have something to do first. Is there any possible way to pick her up tomorrow?" he asked.

"Well, I have one cat in the hospital that will be staying all weekend," I responded. "Could you meet me here at nine o'clock tomorrow morning?"

I knew the boss would not be happy if Mr. Pascal failed to show up and never paid his bill. But the voice on the other end of the phone seemed so sincere. I was willing to take that risk. When I told Paula that Mr. Pascal would be picking up the body in the morning, she gave me a strange look. I assumed that she too worried that my leniency might lead to trouble when the boss came back on Monday morning.

I somehow managed to stumble through the remaining appointments. It was about 1:15 when I finally crossed out the number 1 on the scratch pad. A beautiful June day waited outside, but as we left, all of the employees seemed unusually quiet as we headed for our cars. I assumed that they all were upset at being kept at work longer than usual. I was mentally exhausted and thankful that none of them complained out loud.

On Sunday morning, at nine o'clock sharp, while I was giving an injection to the hospitalized cat, the doorbell rang. I started up a small flight of steps to the front office to answer the bell, and then I froze dead in my tracks. Through the glass door I could see Mr. Pascal. He was looking off to the side and could not see me. I stepped back out of sight as my heart began to race many times faster than yesterday.

For the first time, I realized that I never really had looked at Mr. Pascal the day before. The face at the door was the same, but the entire picture had changed. The man at the door was over six feet tall with dark greasy hair. Both huge arms sported gnarly tattoos. A rounded belly shaded half of a gigantic belt buckle. Sunlight gleamed off the handle of a pistol in a holster hanging from his belt. Behind him in the parking lot sat a huge motorcycle with a black leather jacket draped over the seat. Something large and rectangular was strapped on the back.

I couldn't believe how unobservant I had been. I wrestled between calling the police and keeping my word to this man. Common sense was telling me that I was alone in the building and I should call the police. Over and over, the whimpering telephone voice that loved Susie so much played back in my head. But I also remembered the worried look on Paula's face, and even with closed eyes, I could picture the pistol that I had failed to see yesterday reflected in her eyes. When the bell sounded again, I drew in a deep breath, held it for a moment, exhaled, and headed for the door.

The giant grizzly figure with bloodshot eyes and tear streaks on both cheeks stepped in through the door.

"Thanks, Doc," he said, throwing both arms around me. "I really appreciate you meeting me this morning." I could feel the loss for his pet and the handle of his pistol at the same time. "Doc, Can you help me for a minute? I built Susie a casket last night."

"Sure," I replied, too confused to say anything else, and I followed him out to his bike.

Together, we untied a delicately oiled oak casket and carried it in, placing it gently on the very table where Susie had lain twenty-four hours earlier. I stared in amazement as he loosened a brass latch and opened the piano-hinged box. The inside was lined with red satin and velvet, with perfectly pleated ruffles on all sides. It was a miniature coffin in every sense of the word.

"You built this?" I gasped in amazement. Somehow the pistol became a bit less threatening. "It's beautiful!"

"Yeah … I was up most of the night," he said, wiping moisture from his face with his tattooed forearm. "It's the only way I could try to make this up to Susie."

I brought Susie's lifeless body into the room and spent several minutes helping Mr. Pascal position her as comfortably as possible in the exquisite chamber. Then he handed me cash to pay his bill. When I turned to get change, he insisted on leaving the balance. I accepted it gracefully, telling him it would find its way to the employee coffee fund. We carried Susie carefully out the door and strapped the casket onto the back of the bike.

"Thanks again, Doc, for trying your best," he said as he pulled up a thick zipper on the black leather jacket.

The motorcycle roared out of the parking lot, heading south on the highway. I would never see or hear from Mr. Pascal again, yet I would always remember the lesson learned. I never again judged an owner's level of attachment to his or her pet based on a first impression. As the motorcycle rounded a bend and disappeared from sight, I could feel the warm morning breeze drying unnoticed tears on the side of my face.

CHAPTER 2
New Undergrad Major
Ithaca, 1969-70

I STARED DOWN THE HIGHWAY, long after Mr. Pascal was gone, and mixed emotions stirred within. Had I arrived as an official vet? I knew little about the real world of veterinary medicine. Seated on the stairs leading to the side entrance of the animal hospital, I tried to sort it all out. Rather than focusing on the present, in the bright sunlight and warm morning air, my mind wandered back to the past, to a barbeque party at Cornell University near the end of freshman undergraduate year.

During the summer of 1969, before college, I had noticed Barbara for the first time. I knew she had been in our high school graduating class that year at Kenmore East. But in a school with a senior body of well over 700 students, we had never been in the same classroom, met, or talked. We both were working for the summer at IDS, a department store, and one day I saw her sitting at a table eating lunch with co-workers. Long red hair swept past her shoulders, accenting lightly freckled skin. It made her stand out from the group that day. Ironically, once I learned more, her personality did just the opposite. She had been raised in a family of six children in a small, three-bedroom ranch home only two blocks from my roots, and maybe that had something to do with why her persona was humble, even shy. Something about that shyness charmed me immediately, and I found myself imagining a future with her.

My first attempt to approach her a few days later went poorly. She acted startled, even scared by the attention. I backed off, but I noticed her again

9

and again at work in the days and weeks to come. Determined to continue, I managed to arrange a few activities as a foursome with Barb and two of her friends and co-workers, Leslie and Elaine. Leslie liked me, and I think the girls were all hoping that I would eventually fall for her instead of Barb. And so the games began.

Over the next few weeks, we traveled in a group visiting Sherkston Beach, the amusement park at Crystal Beach, a drive-in movie, a house party, and finally an evening at the Erie County Fair. Barbara could not make it to the fairgrounds, but I went anyway, if only to prove I was playing the game the right way. In the end nothing changed except for the intensity of my interest in Barb.

Determined to continue the quest, I somehow convinced her to go to dinner with me a few days before leaving Buffalo for Ithaca. It was our first official date late in August of 1969. We went to the newest and finest restaurant in the neighborhood, one that was well above either of our means. It might be my only opportunity to win her heart, I thought.

"Oh my, can you believe this?" I asked as the waiter handed us menus painted on a plate of fine china.

"I can barely read it in this candlelight," whispered Barbara.

I was head over heels that night, ready to charge forward, but Barb's reaction was more conservative, more realistic, and more appropriate. She was intrigued by my determination to win her, but she established a firm wall of caution between us. We finished dinner and promised to keep in touch. In reality, I had barely touched her hand, and clearly not her heart. But she had touched mine.

Just days later, I headed off to the College of Agriculture at Cornell University, in Ithaca, New York. Being an outdoor enthusiast, I had chosen wildlife science as a major, hoping in four years time to land a position as a wildlife biologist, a fisheries biologist, or perhaps a park ranger. I was the first in my entire family to go away to a four-year college. As I settled into the freshmen men's dorm on campus, I felt certain of a budding relationship developing back home. That allowed me to distance myself from the behavior of other freshmen men as they explored the freedom of being away from home for the first time. More than a few chased headlong after young women with total reckless and foolish abandon, and it quickly dawned on me that the 150 miles that separated Buffalo from Ithaca and Peter from Barbara was a blessing, not a burden. The distance forced me to proceed at a more appropriate pace.

The separation worked for Barb as well. We began exchanging a couple of letters each week and talked by phone at least once. With each letter and each phone call, the wall between us began to fall, brick by brick by brick. In late October, Barb made the long drive to Ithaca to attend the homecoming football game, and I managed to make it home for a couple of other weekends to spend time with her. The wall continued to crumble. By the time the fall semester was over, it was gone forever.

When I returned home to Buffalo for winter recess, we were both sure that we loved each other and were melting into a oneness that neither of us had ever experienced. We spent our days together and met each other's family. I was touched by how her family accepted me—as if I had been there for years—almost like another sibling. Her large family, living in a small house, graciously made room for one more.

As I learned more about Barb's family, another reality started to seep into my bones. While I was impressed by the fact that I was pursuing a four-year degree at an Ivy League college, Barb's family took it in stride. Many members of her family had college educations, some beyond the undergraduate level. And it had been that way for several generations. As I returned to campus in mid-January, the smallest seed had been planted that maybe I, too, should consider school beyond a four-year program.

As a science major, excellent grades in math and science had always come easily for me. English was a different story, and at Cornell, one more spring semester English course stood in my way. It was a course entitled "Shakespeare and the Moderns," and our first modern assignment was to select a book from *The New York Times* best-seller list, read it, and write a report. I selected *The Making of a Surgeon*, by William Nolen, MD. The book was Dr. Nolen's memoirs of his transformation from a brash medical student to a skilled surgeon as he worked through an internship and residency program at Bellevue Hospital in Manhattan. The stories were told with a touching mixture of humor and humility combined with the realities of the world of medicine. Reading his book at the very moment when I was bored and disenchanted with the freshman curriculum ignited a spark of interest in medicine. Not human medicine, to be sure, but veterinary medicine, combining my interests in animals and medicine.

With Barb now firmly established in my life, everything began to change. I researched what courses I would need to shift majors and what special requirements I would need in order to apply to the veterinary college. I also researched alternative career paths if I failed to get accepted into a vet school. It would be too late to return to wildlife science or any of its related opportunities. Yet I was also determined to stay on a safe path to a secure future and not quite ready to make such a bold and risky move.

That spark of interest in veterinary medicine was flamed in late May, during the academic break between classes and the final exams. The professors in the wildlife science department hosted a picnic for all students in their department. On a sunny and warm day, seated at a picnic table with several seniors in the wildlife science program, I commented about the beautiful weather.

"Not really," replied one of the seniors. "You wouldn't be enjoying it if you were taking ornithology and faced with learning over two hundred birds by their song calls. We have our final early next week, and we need to identify birds by listening to recordings. Every time a bird chirps in these trees, I cringe!"

Despite my intense interest in the outdoors, small birds had never caught my interest. Unique small birds, like hummingbirds, were interesting, but I couldn't name more than one species. Being able to tell a sparrow from a starling or noticing minor variations between different species of finches didn't ignite my imagination.

As I listened to the groans of the senior students, I knew for sure it was time for action. The next morning, I shifted majors from wildlife science to biology in order to accommodate the pre-vet requirements. I still worried that a career in veterinary medicine was a dream that would prove elusive.

However, I was ready to give it my best shot. I planned to pursue a career in research if vet school never materialized. That same day, I scurried around campus finding a new academic advisor, and I selected a professor who was deeply involved in research I could embrace, Dr. Ari van Tienhoven. He had a renowned background in the field of animal reproductive physiology. I was pleased when he agreed to accept me after a brief interview.

"Are you ready for the challenges ahead?" he asked in his prominent Dutch accent.

"I believe so, sir," I responded, parroting what he wanted to hear, but feeling not nearly as certain as I sounded.

CHAPTER 3
Striving for Vet School
Ithaca, early 1970s

IT WASN'T LONG BEFORE BARB AND I were engaged and planning a future together. We managed to arrange to see each other, usually at home in Buffalo, at least once each month. We even played chess by mail that year to stay connected.

For a while that year, I tried to be the quintessential pre-vet student, being active and involved in school-related activities. However, it did not last long, and I remember the moment when I chose to be more selective about my time and loyalties. It happened the night I attended a meeting of the Cornell Pre-Vet Society. While the speaker, a professor from the vet school, was interesting, most of the students attending the meeting were people I realized that I did not wish to emulate. Everyone seemed consumed by their grade point averages and their standing with various professors, but no one seemed remotely realistic about how difficult it would be to get admitted to any veterinary college. I realized two things that evening. First, only one in ten of those students would actually end up in vet school. Second, if I turned out to be one of the nine, I had better have a backup plan. I left that meeting intending to return the following month, but I never did return. I had always been more of a loner that a socialite. The Pre-Vet Society atmosphere that was appropriate for most students simply didn't meld with my approach to life.

After my sophomore year, I returned home to Buffalo in search of a summer job that would give me the hands-on work experiences required for all veterinary students. I knew that if my application was to be taken seriously,

I would need to have experience working with large animals. Fortunately, using the resources of the student placement office in Cornell's College of Agriculture, I found a job on a dairy farm twenty miles from home. It meant working hard for the agriculture minimum wage of $1.50 per hour. But I knew my family's roots had come from dairy farming, and I embraced the opportunity to experience life on a farm, full-time for one summer. It was a large, progressive farm, milking about 125 head of cattle in a modern milking parlor. Mornings were spent working in the fields, harvesting hay and handling chores at the satellite barn where the young stock was being raised. Late each afternoon, I helped with the milking operation.

Barbara and I were married by then, and we both looked forward to moving into an apartment in Ithaca for my junior year of college. Barb had made the decision to abandon her career path to support mine.

The first semester of my junior year was crammed with the most difficult courses to date, but I managed to squeeze in enough requirements by midyear to apply to the Cornell College of Veterinary Medicine. I knew that only a very small number of students were typically admitted after their junior year, but I was determined to start the process. As a senior undergrad, I planned to apply to several veterinary schools in addition to Cornell. This year would be a trial run, helping me understand the process. Applying next year would be my best chance to gain admission somewhere.

In March of my junior year, I was taken by surprise when I was invited to interview for admission to Cornell's veterinary college. As I wandered up to the vet school on upper campus for the appointed interview, I felt numb and blank. I had no idea what to expect, and I regretted not attending more of those Pre-Vet Society meetings.

My jaw dropped and my heart skipped several beats when the secretary directed me into the interview room. There was a chair waiting for me at the end of a long table, and seated around the table were seven people. I was about to be grilled in a group interview, and I hadn't seen any of it coming. I cursed my lack of research and preparation, yet at the same time, I realized that I would have been even more nervous had I known that this was coming. I took a deep breath, sat down, and pretended to relax.

The man at the far end of the table introduced himself as the director of student affairs, and he told me that he was from my hometown.

"I grew up in Tonawanda when there was only one high school, Kenmore High. I see you went to Kenmore East. Who is the principal there now?" His easy questions helped to calm my nerves.

He introduced the others around the table as veterinary professors from various departments. They began asking their questions one by one. Each obviously had my student transcript in front of him or her as several questions related to my undergrad courses. Finally, the last professor, from the ambulatory division of the large animal clinic, was up. One of the tasks of his clinic was to visit Ithaca area dairy farms and treat farm animals on location. He obviously had read a report that I had written on my summer work on the dairy farm.

"What was the average herd milk production on the farm where you worked?" he asked.

My mind felt numb as I couldn't remember anything specific about that report. I took a deep gulp, again cursing my lack of preparation.

"Well, to be honest, I'm not certain," I answered. Then some small recollection jumped into my head. "But I seem to recall that the average milk production in New York State is around fourteen thousand pounds of milk per cow per year. And I know the farm I worked on exceeded the state average comfortably. I believe their herd average was around sixteen thousand pounds per head." My answer was 1 percent recollection and 99 percent speculation.

I walked out of the interview wondering if I had blown it. Had my guess revealed my lack of preparation? When I returned to our apartment, I rummaged through a desk drawer looking for my copy of the report. I relaxed a bit when the numbers spit out an hour earlier were right on the money. I took a few minutes to reread the entire report in preparation for next year.

CHAPTER 4

Brian Michael

Ithaca, September 1971

IT WASN'T LONG BEFORE WE FOUND OURSELVES planning for the arrival of our first child. As a college town, Ithaca had a student population exceeding its permanent population. That made for a community ahead of the curve when it came to ideas about pregnancy care and childbirth. Barb had chosen the largest downtown ob-gyn practice for her care. It had five obstetricians, all male. The practice was affectionately dubbed Fifty Fingers by many of the young female patients. This practice was the leader in the very new idea of allowing fathers to accompany their wives into the delivery room. With one exception. One older doctor still refused to allow husbands entrance. Because the five doctors rotated coverage for deliveries, fathers had a four in five chance of being in the delivery room, but they had no sure guarantee of it.

We did not have maternity coverage on our health insurance at that time, so the obstetrician's fees and the hospital fees needed to be paid out of pocket. We had a small amount of money set aside to cover the costs. Two weeks before the scheduled delivery I was asked to deliver a $500 payment to the hospital. An understanding hospital clerk accepted my check. She was a young woman, and she clearly had compassion for students about to be faced with some steep hospital bills. She gave me great advice about how the system worked.

"Many couples don't know this, but almost all of the ob-gyns in town will discharge the mother and baby two days after delivery rather than three days if everything is going well and if you ask," she said. "If that happens, we send you a seventy-five dollar refund check in the mail. But there's one more thing. Hospital billing often confuses people. Each day counts as a day no matter how short a time you spend in the hospital. If you check in before midnight, it counts as a day. I try to make sure everyone knows how the billing works ahead of time. It prevents a lot of misunderstandings later."

"Thanks," I said, acknowledging how little I knew about the financial arrangements.

As Barbara's due date drew near, she became restless. We talked about names for the baby. If it was a girl, we were in clear agreement about a name. It would be Leanne Jeanette. But we never were able to feel certain about a boy's name. Barb had a list of five names but had not made a final choice. It made no difference to me; they all seemed fine. When the due date arrived and passed, Barb turned to cleaning everything in the house over and over again. I had classes to keep me occupied, but she was on maternity leave and had nothing else to bide her time as she waited for relief from the discomfort of the final days of a pregnancy. I tried my best to understand her restlessness, and I quickly learned to stay out of her way. By the fifth day past her due date, she was miserable. It was a Friday, and I only had one class in the morning. When I returned home, she was cleaning again.

"Hey, it's a beautiful day out there," I said wanting to take her mind off of everything. "Let's take a ride down to Stewart Park and wander around."

At the park we watched the white-tailed deer that were on display in a small enclosure. We watched other young couples with their toddlers feeding ducks. We knew we would be back in a year or two doing the same. Barb's back was sore and she wanted to go home. She was acting differently, too, so I sensed things might finally start to move forward.

When we arrived at the apartment, she decided to bake some cookies. It seemed to be a strange time for such activity, but I at least knew not to argue with a woman at a moment like this. It was better than cleaning the same things one more time. Soon she had a huge bowl of cookie dough ready. Having been raised in a family with six children, the idea of making a single batch of anything never occurred to her. Judging by the size of that bowl of dough, it appeared she was preparing to have several children that night and that they would return home the next day ready for cookies. She put the bowl of dough in the refrigerator, planning to bake them after dinner. But the bowl never moved.

By seven o'clock, it was clear that her back pain was morphing into labor pain. By nine o'clock, I was on the phone with the ob-gyn answering service. Unfortunately, Dr. No-Husbands was on call that night, but at that moment it didn't matter; we just wanted it over. Soon, the doctor's grumpy voice called back, and we talked.

"Not quite yet," he said, "but get ready." We talked again about 11:25, and finally I heard, "Pack up and head for the hospital."

We pulled into Tompkins County Hospital about ten minutes before midnight. Barb was between contractions, so I suggested that we sit in the car and chat a little before going into the hospital. I had one eye on my watch and the other on her belly. We talked about how wonderful it was going to be to start our family and how unfortunate it was that I would not be allowed into the delivery room. Then I pulled out the list of boys' names to review once again.

"If it's a boy, pick any one. They're all fine with me," I repeated one last time.

Then another contraction started. I held her tightly. When the pain passed, I gave her a kiss, and I looked at my watch. Midnight. A new day. And we headed for the hospital entrance. She knew absolutely nothing about the seventy-five dollars her manipulative husband had just saved.

For the next five hours, I was imprisoned in the father's waiting room, pacing and waiting. It didn't seem bad. This was the way it worked in every movie and on every television drama I'd ever seen. There was one other father in the room that night. He was twice my age, awaiting his fourth child. He couldn't imagine why any husband would want to be in the delivery room. About four in the morning, his wife delivered a healthy baby girl, and I was alone.

Finally, at 5:20 AM, Dr. No-Husbands came into the room, shook my hand, and told me I had a healthy son. His hand and his eyes were as warm as an ice cube. It was clear that heading home for some sleep was far more important than congratulating some young, snotty college student, but it didn't matter. I had a son. And my son and Barb were doing well.

Twenty minutes later, a nurse rolled Barb out of the delivery room, and I was allowed to meet her in the hallway. She smiled as she showed me our little baby hidden inside his blanket. Her eyes told me how happy she was. Her hair, however, told me more than I wanted to know about what had transpired during the delivery. Her gorgeous, long red hair was twisted and snarled up into several huge knots. If it had not been for the smile, the rosy cheeks, and the sparkling eyes, I might not have recognized her. For the first time, the reality of not being in the room hit home. If only I could have held her hand and encouraged her through the torture she had just endured. Maybe I could have helped prevent the mess on her head. If the bird's nest of tangle had been on one of my fishing reels, I would have cut the line away and started over. I wondered if she would want to do the same. It took her two days to comb her hair out, and she said it was the second most painful thing she ever experienced.

Before they rolled her away, I gave her another kiss, peeked at the little boy wrapped in a blanket, and asked her if she'd selected a name. She had chosen Brian Michael. I told her I would call both sets of parents and give them the news.

I headed straight for the pay phone with a pocketful of quarters that had been waiting patiently all night. I called my parents first and my father answered.

"You and Mom have your first grandson!" I announced. "His name is Brian Michael. He weighed in at eight pounds, six ounces. Both the baby and Barb are doing fine."

Dad dutifully wrote everything down for the rest of the family.

As the story goes, a couple of hours later, when my younger brother, Doug, got out of bed and went to the kitchen, he saw the note on the table and gasped.

"I know my brother is at an Ivy League college. But why is he so conceited that he named his first son *Brain*?"

Dyslexia is common in our family. Even though conditions like that were never diagnosed in his day, there was never a question about Dad's dyslexia.

22

As a mechanic, he could dismantle several automatic transmissions, rebuild them, and put the hundreds of parts back together without losing a piece and without written instructions. But like most dyslexics, myself included, his spelling was not good, and he often reversed letters and numbers. Brian had morphed into Brain.

In a way, it would have been fun to be there and see the look on Doug's face as he read the note. But I was 150 miles away. I was in Ithaca. I was with my wife. I was a father. I was getting an education for myself *and* for my family. I was on top of the world!

Suddenly, a muffled roar in the distance caught my attention. It grew louder and louder, and abruptly I returned to reality as a group of six huge motorcycles roared by on the highway. I could feel the warmth from the metallic band of my wristwatch that was baking in the morning sunshine. Realizing I had been sitting on the steps of the animal hospital daydreaming, I glanced down. It was almost half past ten. I had been sitting there for more than an hour after helping Mr. Pascal load his handmade casket with Susie's body onto the back of his motorcycle. It was going to be a hot afternoon. I stood up and headed home.

CHAPTER 5
First Solo Surgery
West Seneca, June 1976

THE NEXT MORNING THE STAFF WAS fascinated by the story from the prior day.

"Wow! That guy looked really scary on Saturday morning," said Paula as we talked about the motorcycle and casket. "You just never know about people. Do you?"

With Dr. Tom, the hospital owner, back in the office, my stress of handling the practice alone eased for the moment. Unfortunately, the relief proved to be very brief. Tuesday marked my first turn to handle surgery. I noticed that ten surgeries were scheduled for the day, but I was too stubborn or too proud to admit that ten surgeries were more than I was ready to handle. My surgical experience during college had consisted of less than a dozen surgeries spread out over a two-year period. At the university level, in an academic setting, all of my surgery experience had been tightly supervised. There was always an experienced surgeon to guide students through each procedure. Furthermore, multiple surgeries were never scheduled back-to-back to avoid time pressure. Many of the other third-year veterinary students gained additional experience working during the summer in outside practices in their hometowns, where they were allowed to perform minor surgeries or assist in major surgeries. However, since Barb and I were married with children, it had not been feasible for us to pull up stakes and return home to Buffalo, where a summer assignment might have been possible. Instead, I had spent my summers working on a poultry farm in the Ithaca area. Needless to say, on that Tuesday morning at Dr. Tom's clinic, I was still an extremely green surgeon about to fly solo for the first time.

Normally, the technicians admitted patients early in the morning. The surgeon was expected to arrive at 8:30 to begin the first procedure. I promised to arrive early, ready to be helpful and to begin as soon as possible. A few minutes past eight, Paula had the first cat under anesthesia and prepped for surgery. Sheila, our other technician, would admit the remaining pets. Sheila was quite different from Paula. Raised by a single father, a lumberjack, in a rural area well south of Buffalo, she was short of stature but tough of spirit; hard work was her lifestyle. Despite their different styles and personalities, Sheila and Paula worked seamlessly together.

Cat surgeries are typically first as they are a bit easier than dog surgeries. Cats are smaller, they tend to bleed less, and also they recover more slowly from anesthesia. Doing cat surgeries first allows better monitoring during the recovery phase.

While the surgeries proceeded smoothly, I was experiencing unexpected difficulty seeing all the internal tissues of the animals. The surgery room had recently been renovated, and so far, there were no special surgical lights over the table. Only fluorescent bulbs in the ceiling lit the surgical field. Dr. Tom's eyesight must have been sharper than mine. I made a mental note to ask permission to move proper surgical lighting into this room. I also decided that it was time to make an appointment for an eye exam to see if I needed glasses in surgery.

Despite the dim light, we finished three cat surgeries by 9:30. Things were going much smoother than expected, and the first dog was ready to be spayed. This pooch was small, the surgery progressed nicely, and her incision was closed by a few minutes past ten.

With growing confidence, I started surgery on a much larger dog, Patti, also to be spayed. Spaying requires removal of both ovaries and the uterus, and the larger the dog, the more difficult the procedure. A longer incision is needed, and the organs are deep inside the body cavity, much harder to reach.

My first stroke of the scalpel cut neatly through the skin. Dogs have thick skin compared to humans, but scalpel blades are razor sharp. One pass of the blade generally opens the skin revealing fatty tissue below, and minor bleeding is easily controlled. Next, with a second lighter stroke of the scalpel, I parted the fatty tissue revealing the muscles of the abdominal wall. I gently scraped the fat away from the muscles so that I could see the line separating the two major muscle groups on either side of the abdomen. Then I passed the scalpel along that line, opening the abdomen.

The entire inside of the abdominal cavity is lined with a smooth, tough layer called the peritoneum. This layer protects the muscles on the outside while creating a smooth and slippery layer inside, allowing free movement of the intestines. In the dim light, I could see a glistening layer, and I poked at it with my finger. I decided that the last cut had not passed through the peritoneum. One more stroke of the blade would be necessary to enter the abdomen.

I quickly swiped the scalpel along the gleaming surface, and I panicked as an eruption of fluid splashed out of the incision. Immediately it was apparent that I had misidentified the gleaming surface. The abdomen had already been opened with the prior cut, so my scalpel had cut into the wall of the urinary bladder. Urine was flowing all over the surgical field. Beneath the surgical mask, my lips trembled and beads of perspiration erupted on my forehead.

When a pet is prepared for abdominal surgery, the technicians have a set routine. They administer an initial anesthesia by injection and then insert a tube into the windpipe, connecting the patient to the gas anesthesia machine. This tube delivers oxygen and anesthetic gas to the patient. Next the hair is clipped and shaved from the abdomen, where the incision will soon be made. Then, with gentle pressure, the bladder is expressed, removing any excess urine. Finally, the area is scrubbed with antiseptic soap to kill any germs on the skin. Emptying the bladder is an important part of preparation for surgery because an enlarged bladder can hinder the surgeon's view.

Sheila and Paula had forgotten to empty the bladder. Patti's bladder was so fully distended that its smooth surface filled the incision area, resembling the lining of the abdomen. Both technicians realized what had happened at the same time I did, and they were staring at me and each other in terror. They expected me to scream about their oversight. Skilled surgeons are often quick-tempered and explode in anger when things go poorly. However, I was anything but a skilled surgeon, and I knew that my error was the true cause of this situation. I had parlayed their oversight into a crisis. Any seasoned surgeon would have recognized the bladder wall and worked around the obstacle. There was no benefit to blaming my surgical inexperience on the technicians.

"Damn," I proclaimed, "I can't believe I did something that stupid!"

In a healthy bladder, urine is sterile, so the risk of infection is low. But the risk of irritation is high.

"Paula, grab some chromic gut suture right away," I said. "Sheila, warm up some IV fluids. We need something to dilute and flush the urine from the incision," I said trying to stay calm and sound confident.

Fortunately, one of the surgical procedures I had performed as a senior veterinary student was called a cystotomy. In that procedure, we had learned how to open a bladder to remove stones or growths inside and then how to repair the bladder wall, as well as how to handle the urine spills. I began to repair the damage I had done, hoping that I was remembering each required step. First I enlarged the incision and gently pulled most of the bladder outside of the body cavity to inspect the wound. Then I sutured the wall of the bladder to repair the cut. I rinsed the bladder thoroughly with warm sterile fluids, and after examining and testing the suture line several times to make sure the seal was not leaking, I carefully lowered the bladder back into the abdomen. Next I flushed the entire incision area with fluids to wash away remnants of urine. Finally I was able to locate and remove the uterus and ovaries so that the spay surgery was completed.

The entire procedure took almost two hours. Sheila and Paula did everything asked of them, but they were stone silent the entire time, apparently still expecting to take the blame for the error.

"I'm really sorry ladies," I said as we carried Patti from surgery. "My inexperience caused this problem. It's not your fault."

We plodded through the next surgery, and we finally finished all ten procedures by two o'clock in the afternoon. Two hours late was somehow acceptable given the complication encountered.

As I headed to my first afternoon office call after the final surgery, the muscles in my lower back felt like Jell-O. I had bent over the surgical table for almost six hours straight. Interestingly, I hadn't noticed the growing discomfort during the hours of surgery, but now my muscles sagged and begged for relief. We had all missed lunch as well, although I don't think any of us could have eaten at that point anyway.

A smooth layer of tissue called mucosa covers the internal organs, including the bladder. This type of tissue grows and repairs itself very rapidly. Once Patti had recovered from surgery, Sheila and Paula made sure that she walked outside every hour that afternoon, giving the bladder a chance to heal without undue pressure on the sutures. The bladder wound was probably sealed within hours of the surgery, but it would take far longer for my wounded ego to heal.

Never once did I mention that the bladder had not been emptied, especially in Dr. Tom's presence. In that one brief hour of surgical crisis, Sheila and Paula formed an invisible bond with me, the new Doc on staff. By accepting the blame for all of us, I think I earned their silent but lasting respect. That bond would prove to be a priceless asset in the struggles ahead.

I drove back to the hospital twice that night to take Patti out for a walk, once at three in the morning. Mercifully, no blood appeared in her urine, and she showed no signs of discomfort. She was on the road to a complete recovery.

As I tossed and turned that night, my thoughts again returned to the path we had taken to arrive in West Seneca. It was the only way to think about something other than the surgical error from that morning.

CHAPTER 6

The Letter

AFTER BRIAN WAS BORN, things began to move forward more rapidly. In no time at all, it was late spring of my junior year, and students would soon learn who had been accepted into vet school and who had been rejected. One day in microbiology lab, two of the students were crowing about receiving letters of congratulations from the veterinary college. A larger group of students was watching them, and they all looked like they had been hit by a train. They apparently knew they had not made the cut. Since I hadn't heard anything, I assumed the letters of acceptance had gone out first, and the letters of rejection would follow soon. I was reminded of how few applicants to vet school actually got accepted, and I reminded myself that, as a junior, I certainly never stood a chance of being one of them. Most of these classmates didn't even know that I had applied to vet school, so I stayed out of the conversation.

Four days later, as I returned to our apartment from campus, I plucked the mail from our mailbox and descended the steps to our basement apartment. As I flicked through the pile, I noticed a letter with a return address from the New York State College of Veterinary Medicine at Cornell. Barb was seated at the kitchen table reading a magazine. Brian was sound asleep in his crib in the tiny room off that kitchen that we had converted into a nursery. Since Barb and I both liked to tease each other about weird things, I tossed the envelope on the table in front of her.

"Here, you open my letter of rejection!" I quipped as I turned and headed

31

for the living room.

"You idiot!" she screamed moments later. "This is a letter of acceptance!"

I had always been the self-proclaimed king of good-natured teasing, so I generally could accept being the target as well as the shooter. But this was simply too mean, and I winced as she mouthed the words.

The next thing I knew, she sprang from the chair, jumped onto my back, almost knocking me over. The remaining mail in my hands fell, fluttering to the floor. She spun me around and hugged and kissed me face-to-face. It took a moment to sink in, but as Barbara's warm tears spread to my face, I realized that this was no joke. In no time at all, my tears were mixing with hers, and her long red hair was plastered against my face. Try as I might, there was no way to read the letter in her hand. As her arms pulled tightly around me, I felt her emotion and her pride. Life was about to change in so many ways.

Eventually, we relaxed our grip on each other. Barbara pushed back her hair and tried to wipe some of the moisture from her face. Back at the kitchen table, she sat down and squinted to read the rest of the letter. My every instinct was to grab the letter from her and read it first. But I had started this by tossing the letter to her, and now she deserved the honor.

"We are pleased to inform you …" Barbara started in a cracking voice, realizing I would want to hear every word in the letter.

As she read out loud, I knelt down to pick up the rest of the mail from the floor. Among the mail was the empty envelope from the veterinary college. I looked at it closely. It was battered and dirty. And it was postmarked five days earlier.

"Look," I said as Barb finished reading. "This envelope must have gotten lost somewhere at the post office for the last few days."

We could hear Brian stirring in his crib just a few feet away. If only the envelope could talk and tell the story of the last four days. Then I realized it didn't matter. The story of the next four years would soon be far more important than the story of the last four days. And this totally unexpected acceptance had given me the opportunity to write that story.

Chapter 7
Zap, Crackle, Pop
Ithaca, Summer 1972

ONCE I HAD RECEIVED THE VET SCHOOL ACCEPTANCE, Barb and I were on cloud nine. The days between the arrival of the acceptance letter and the beginning of the grind of medical classes provided a wonderful interlude. We were showered with congratulations from family, friends, and classmates.

Soon we were both hard at work making adjustments. Knowing we would be in Ithaca for another four years, our first priority was better housing. The university offered married-student apartments on upper campus, close to the vet school, and we put our names on the waiting list. Next I started to apply for student loans. With both of us working, we had avoided any loans to date, but that needed to change. We also both decided to look for better jobs. Barb was comfortable in her job working as a retail clerk at an army-navy surplus store downtown, but it was time to aim for something better. She started brushing up her typing skills, preparing for a test on campus. There were many opportunities for secretarial positions if she could make the grade. I was working part-time in the Ag school library but wondered if I could parlay the acceptance to veterinary school into a more meaningful summer position.

At the student placement office, while pawing through a stack of cards describing opportunities in the Ithaca area, one position jumped out. It was a field technician for the research arm of the Entomology department. The job description called for a student to handle the fieldwork in a project studying fly control on area dairy farms. That sounded more interesting than being

33

stuck in a library all summer long, so I set up an appointment with the head lab technician at one of Cornell's research facilities not far from campus. The facility was dedicated to entomology—the study of insects. The head technician explained the nature of the study and asked quite a few questions about my ability to socialize with dairy farmers. He explained that there was often a disconnect between area farmers and some of the research arms of the Ag school. The farmers often viewed the researchers, and especially the professors who designed the research projects, to be ivory tower intellectuals who no longer understood anything about the realities of life down on the farm. This position was officially a field technician for the study, but it was also about being a public relations ambassador for the university. Since our family had come from a dairy farming background, and I had worked on a dairy farm the prior summer, and mostly because I was about to start vet school, he felt I was a perfect fit for the job. He hired me two days later.

A few weeks later, the academic year ended and I reported for work. The head technician issued me a pickup truck and rode along for the first two days. He introduced me to the farmers and explained the research project that was already underway. There were twelve farms in the study, all relatively small. Six of them were control farms. That meant they weren't allowed to use any form of fly control in or around their barns. The other six farms were treatment farms. A chemical, an organophosphate pesticide, was mixed into the grain that the cows ate on these farms. It was a pesticide that was supposed to stay in the intestinal track and not be absorbed into the bloodstream. It moved through the digestive system and passed out of the cows in their manure.

Fly problems on farms are worse than almost anywhere else because of the fly's life cycle. Flies lay their eggs in rotting organic matter, commonly in manure, the quintessential organic matter that is never in short supply around livestock. The eggs hatch out into larvae—most of us call them maggots. After a short period of feeding, the larvae form small cocoonlike structures called pupae. Soon new adult flies emerge from the pupae just as butterflies emerge from a cocoon. The goal of the study was to see if the pesticide residue in the manure would break the life cycle of the flies, preventing the larvae from developing.

In order to monitor the fly population in the various barns, small one-inch strips of typing paper were thumbtacked to the barn ceilings in ten different locations around each barn. Once each week, I collected the old strips of paper and replaced them with new strips. Back inside the lab, bench technicians examined the strips under dissecting microscopes, counting each and every mark of fly spittle on the paper. The more spots found on the paper, the higher the population, yielding a scientific measurement of the fly density in each barn on a weekly basis.

I also learned other minor responsibilities, like measuring out and taking the actual powdered chemical to the feed mill where the grain was ground to see that it was mixed properly with the food. All in all, however, there was not a whole lot of work to do. Much of my time was spent visiting with the farmers, making certain they were comfortable with their role in the study. If even one farm opted to drop out during of the summer, the entire study might be compromised. In all, the job appeared to be 10 percent field technician and 90 percent public relations.

I was just getting comfortable in the position when the job suddenly became 1 percent technician and 99 percent public relations. In mid-June, the remnants of Hurricane Agnes deposited record amounts of rainfall on the Finger Lakes region of New York State. Historic floods were recorded in nearby Elmira and Corning as the Chemung River overflowed its banks. Waters rose to the point where the famous glass museum in Corning had five feet of water—and the museum was housed on the second floor. Barb became very busy as the army-navy store had its headquarters and warehouse in Elmira, and all of their merchandise was underwater. As soon as the floodwaters receded, the store began to ship truck after truck of wet clothing to Ithaca, where everything was sold out of piles in the parking lot at a dollar apiece for any item.

The farm fields around the Ithaca area were saturated to the point where none of the normal field work was possible—and right at the peak of haying season. But farmers are a resilient lot. They take everything in stride. I couldn't stop at a farm without being invited in for a huge breakfast or massive lunch.

Or to play cards or checkers for an hour or so—while the rains poured down. Getting to know the farmers and making friends was nothing but fun. I was getting paid to gain weight. By the time the fields dried out, I was a good friend with each and every farm family in the group of twelve.

Shortly after the fields dried, our first problem arose. Three cows on two different treatment farms aborted late-term calves with serious birth defects. All three were dead. One was even a grotesque one-eyed cyclops. It may have been mere coincidence that all three cases were among the cows eating the chemically laced feed, but it seemed obvious to me that all three should go to the veterinary college for autopsies and toxicology studies. I checked with the lab for permission to cover the costs, and it was granted all three times, although not without a few strange looks along the way. A big-name chemical company was funding the study, and while no one said anything, it seemed to me that there was subtle pressure in corporate-sponsored research not to make waves. All three autopsies found no problems and no residues of the pesticide, which made me feel more comfortable with the study protocol. Yet I could picture my name and photo on a bulletin board in the chemical company's research department with the words *Avoid This Guy* written below.

Late in the summer, the professor in charge of the entire lab called me into his office. He pointed to a large box on the floor next to his desk.

"Do you have any control barns where the flies are really bad?" he asked. "Some guy just sent me this contraption and wants my opinion. He just applied for a patent on this thing."

In the box was the first prototype fly zapper. It was made with two concentric cylinders of screen with large square openings—eighth-inch hardware cloth ⊠- the kind of screening you might use to build the floor in a rabbit cage. One cylinder was about one-half inch in diameter larger than the other and was outside of it. In the middle were two ultraviolet fluorescent tubes. There were some electrical connections at the top. It was easy for both of us to understand at a glance how this thing would work. Insects see further into the ultraviolet range than humans. Flies would be attracted to the ultraviolet light day or night and then be electrocuted as they flew through any hole in the screening trying to reach the source of the light.

"As a matter of fact, the flies on the Schwartz farm are terrible," I responded. "Mr. Schwartz likes to exaggerate. He keeps telling me he needs to carry a baseball bat with him for protection when he milks. I'm planning to fumigate the place tomorrow right after lunch to give him some relief."

"Perfect! It's a nice afternoon to get out of the building. Let's go out there and try this thing out," the scholarly professor dressed in a business suit responded.

The control farms were designed to study how fast the fly population would increase if no effort was made to control them. It was my job to stall off the farmers as long as possible, then fumigate the barn while the cows were out on pasture to return the base fly population to near zero. The fewer times this happened over the course of the summer, the easier the scientific data would be to interpret. Since Hurricane Agnes had allowed me to become great friends with the farmers, I was able to squeeze every last day of patience from them to cooperate with the study.

The Schwartz farm was the type of old family farm that was rapidly disappearing in the northeast. In fact, it was almost a museum on the history of dairy farming. The husband and wife operating the farm were in their late sixties, with no children to carry on. They milked twenty-five head of Brown Swiss cows. No one milked that few cows anymore. Most farms were passing the hundred-head mark. And virtually no one was milking this rather small breed of cows. The vast majority of dairy farms had shifted to bigger, more familiar, black-and-white Holsteins twenty years earlier because of their higher milk production. The barn was antiquated as well. The stanchions were wooden rather than metal, and the manure gutter was still cleaned by hand. The only things this farm needed were wooden milking stools and maids-a-milking to make it a museum.

Mr. Swartz did use older-model automated milking machines but still poured the milk from each milking through cheesecloth filters into old-fashioned milk cans carried to the milk house, just as my great uncle had done during my childhood. The money the Schwartz's received from Cornell for participating in the study was allowing them to hang on for one more year.

"This ridiculous study is allowing the hands of the big clock to go around one more time for us," Mr. Swartz liked to say. He and his wife were the salt of the earth.

We arrived on the farm about four in the afternoon. The flies were horrific in the barn, and I felt guilty for making this farmer suffer for so long. He was just starting to milk the first two cows. I reassured him that the barn would be fumigated tomorrow after lunch. I told him we were going to try out this new device for a few minutes, and then I headed to the far end of the barn. There were two reasons for using the far end of the barn. One was to try not to disturb the farmer or the cows he was milking. The other was to keep the professor dressed in his shirt and tie as far away from the expletives coming from the farmer attired in tattered coveralls. Most of the farmer's sputtering comments were about Cornell and their crazy studies.

I spotted a nail sticking out of a rafter in the ceiling close to an electrical outlet and hung the zapper. What happened next almost defied description. While we knew the device would electrocute flies, we had no inkling how much noise it might make or what kind of sparks might fly. The instructions on the side of the box gave strong warnings not to touch the screening while it was plugged in. This prototype machine had the full force of 120 volts charging the grids. I stretched the cord over to the electrical outlet, plugged it in, and within seconds, the worst lightning storm of the entire summer of 1972 erupted inside the barn. The crackling and sparks from hundreds, perhaps thousands, of suicidal flies barreling toward the ultraviolet bulbs was incredible. I pulled the plug out as fast as possible, but the damage was done. Every cow in the barn was going crazy. Two cows on our end of the barn had broken out of their wooden stanchions and were staggering around nervously. Naturally, Mr. Swartz was furious. The words from his mouth were almost as bad as the effects of the zapper. I was thankful that the baseball bat he joked about was all talk. We apologized over and over. Abandoning the machine, we beat a retreat to the pickup truck. The professor was worried that we had poisoned our relationship with Mr. Schwartz and had lost possession of someone else's prototype device in his barn.

"Don't worry," I said trying to repress a smile. "I know him well. He has a bit of a temper and had every right to explode. But he's a great guy and will calm down in no time. I'll call him tonight and assure him that Cornell will pay for the damages. I'll retrieve that zapper device tomorrow."

A few hours later I was on the phone, laughing with Mr. Schwartz. As I expected, everything was fine and the repairs were already completed.

"I'll be there right after lunch tomorrow," I promised one more time. "But I'm really intrigued by that strange contraption. Can you do me a favor? After you turn the cows out to pasture in the morning, plug that darn thing in and close up the barn. Let's see what it does by noon."

As I pulled into the farm the following day, Mr. Schwartz was standing outside the milk house. He spotted my pickup and started frantically waving me over. My heart sank. Had my unauthorized instructions caused a problem? Had it blown an electrical circuit or worse yet started a fire?

"Hurry up—you gotta see this!" he urged.

We walked into the barn. Most of the flies were gone. At the far end hung the zapper, still crackling away and spewing out a mini-electric indoor storm. As we walked toward the machine, my eyes widened. I felt a bit like a fly being drawn toward the ultraviolet light. But as we drew closer, my gaze migrated down to the floor below the machine. There was a virtual mountain of scorched dead fly parts at least two feet across and ten inches high

"How many flies do you think this thing killed?" asked Mr. Schwartz.

I had absolutely no idea.

"Millions and millions would be my guess," I said shaking my head. "Who knows? Maybe billions!"

"This thing is great! Can I keep it to use after the study?" asked the farmer.

"No, unfortunately, it doesn't belong to Cornell and has to be returned," I answered. "But I think if the guy who came up with this idea makes a few simple modifications, we'll see these things on the market soon."

That afternoon, I returned to the lab, anxious to tell all my co-workers the story. After finishing, I knocked on the professor's office door. He invited me in. As I tried to tell him the story, he interrupted me in midsentence.

"Just send that damn thing back. I already mailed the guy a letter and told him it's a stupid idea," he stammered.

I wanted to protest but did not. It wasn't my place to challenge a world-renowned professor. So I retreated to the hallway with the box and followed instructions. In a couple of weeks, classes would be starting. Barb and I had moved into our married-student apartment. There were many families with young children, so we knew it would be great for Brian. Barb had started a new secretarial job in the Cornell Hotel School. The student loans were approved. It had been a great summer, and I had thoroughly enjoyed mixing with the farmers. But I was ever so thankful that my career in research had been short-lived. From that day forward, I have smiled every time I spotted a fly zapper glowing in someone's yard.

THE ACADEMIC RIGORS OF VETERINARY SCHOOL already seemed a blur. The class load in vet school was much heavier than my undergrad years, and memorization was nonstop. But school was a different grind. For the most part, the intense focus on having excellent grades was no longer the highest priority. As long as we passed each subject, we kept moving forward. We were given numerical grades in every course, but no numbers appeared on our test papers. Everything was marked S, W, or U—Satisfactory, Warning, or Unsatisfactory. As long as Ss kept showing up, and we didn't get "winged" (a W), we could concentrate more on learning and less on grades.

One decision I had to make early in my freshman year involved whether or not to join a fraternity. There were two veterinary fraternities, and traditionally almost everyone joined one or the other. But change was in the air. The doors of veterinary medicine had always been all but closed for women, but they were quickly beginning to swing open. Cornell admitted 65 first-year students annually. The class one year ahead of mine had four women, and my class had eight. The next class had fourteen women, and by the time I graduated, the incoming class was fast approaching a 50 percent male-to-female ratio.

It was interesting to hear the buzz about how the fraternities would have to reinvent and redesign themselves to adjust to the realities of women in the veterinary school. As a result of the uncertainty and evolving change, there were a small but growing number of students who declined to join either fraternity. I was among them. Being married with a child, I found it less important in my life than my family, and besides, my decision was consistent with the approach I had taken as an undergrad. But it also created a bit of a problem. All veterinary students were required to work outside the college for four hundred hours with large animals and four hundred hours with small animals by the beginning of our third year. One of the work requirements had to be finished before admission, and I had completed that task working on the dairy farm two summers earlier. However, since Barb had a job in the Hotel School and was already working her way up to a position as a departmental secretary, leaving Ithaca for a summer job elsewhere was not an option. My biggest problem was that most of the positions working with small animals in the veterinary college and elsewhere around campus seemed to be controlled by who knew whom in the two fraternities.

Fortunately, I made good friends with John, a fellow freshman who had grown up on a dairy farm outside Rochester. John was in a similar position, needing his small animal experience but also needing to return to his own family farm each summer. It turned out that he knew the ins and outs of the school requirements better than I did, and he told me about a little-known job that did meet the small animal requirement—working on a poultry farm. It was a relic on the books from the days when the veterinary colleges needed to graduate more food animal vets than small animal vets, but it was still there. John told me about Babcock Poultry, a breeder farm that shipped fertilized eggs and newly hatched chicks all over the world. They were located in nearby Trumansburg, and they were expanding rapidly, hiring part-time employees. He applied for a job first and then gave me a heads-up the following day. I followed suit. We were both hired as part-time weekend farm hands, collecting eggs from breeder chickens. John was assigned to their new production farm—twelve brand-new, state-of-the-art buildings that could house twenty thousand chickens each. I was assigned to one of their older production barns several miles away. The feeders were automated, but the eggs were still collected and packed by hand. Every weekend for the next few months, I spent my time learning the basics of the poultry industry. After the Christmas holidays, my assignment changed. The old barn was permanently shut down, and I was moved to the new production farm complex where my friend was working.

The new production complex was quite different as about two dozen employees reported daily to one office, where a manager sent everyone out on assignments. As soon as the manager learned that I was interested in working full time in the summer, he offered me a position as weekend supervisor of the facility along with a modest pay raise. It seemed bizarre that I would be in charge of employees, some of whom were twice my age, but money was tight, so I accepted the position without hesitation. I knew the opportunity was offered to me rather than John because he would not be available in the summer and perhaps would not work past his four-hundred-hour requirement.

I quickly realized I was given the opportunity because the manager found me to be a successful student with good work ethic. He sensed I would be dependable every weekend. It did not take long for me to figure out the realities of managing unskilled farm hands, either. A handful of the employees turned out to be alcoholics, and I typically had to oversee several of them each weekend. They received their paychecks on Friday morning and usually failed to show up for work on Saturday or at best were several hours late. Eighty percent of the eggs were laid within two hours of sunup. John and I were always on time, and we ran around like chickens with our heads cut off, trying our best to keep up with the hens until the AWOL employees staggered in to help. I wouldn't have been able to keep up without John's help.

By spring break, I finally had weekends down to a system, and I was also working some extra hours during the school recess. One time, on a Friday after the paychecks were handed out, a group of the alcoholics invited me to lunch. It seemed worthwhile to join them to see if I could understand them better or find a way to get them to show up earlier on Saturday. We went to a nearby neighborhood saloon and sat on bar stools rather than at a table. This place felt familiar to me. My grandparents had operated a tavern outside of Buffalo in my youth, and the bartender looked a bit like my grandfather. However, the conversations that day were anything but familiar. Two of the employees sitting next to me were a married couple, and I quickly realized that they were both alcoholics. I ordered a sandwich and a Coke, and watched in amazement as the bartender turned to them. Before ordering anything, they signed their paychecks and handed them over. The barkeeper made a few notations in a small book behind the counter, placed their checks in the cash register, and gave them each a twenty-dollar bill. I was stunned to realize how badly they were entrenched in a world they might never escape. I should have been paying Babcock Poultry to work that day. You can't buy lessons in life like that one. Each of the co-workers tried to buy me a drink that day, but I declined politely, and I never went to lunch with them again.

While I was in vet school, it seemed like each academic semester dragged slowly on, but in retrospect, time passed quickly. Midway through my second year, Barbara was pregnant again, and we planned for the arrival of our second child early in my third year. I was busy working at the chicken farm and carrying the heavy workload of junior year when her due date arrived. Once again, the day came and went without signs of labor. And true to form, several days later, her back pain and contractions started. Barb's new obstetrician advised us to report to the hospital, so we took our son Brian to the neighbor's home, and we headed out. This time, I was going to be allowed into the delivery room.

At the hospital, the emergency room nurse examined Barb.

"You are just having false labor. Just back pain from the pregnancy," she announced.

"No way," winced Barb. "It's exactly like my first labor!"

But a pelvic exam revealed no dilation. The doctor on call decided to admit her for observation.

"You look absolutely exhausted," the nurse said to me. "Go home and get some sleep. We'll call as soon as any real labor begins."

I was dog-tired from both school and work, and I decided to follow her advice to catch a few winks. I drove home but left Brian with the neighbors rather than disturb everyone else's sleep. I kicked my shoes off, and crawled onto our bed, fully dressed and ready to return to the hospital on a moments notice.

At some point, I heard ringing off in the distance. It would start and then stop. Later it would start and then stop all over again, a bit louder each time.

Finally, I jolted awake and realized that the telephone was ringing and ringing. When I finally grabbed the phone, and stammered a sleepy hello, the nurse on the other end spoke quickly in an angered tone.

"Your wife is close to delivery," she snapped. "We've been trying to call you for a couple of hours!"

I raced to the hospital as rapidly as possible, but when I ran into the obstetrics hall, a different nurse was wheeling Barb out of the delivery room, with a new son in her arms. Her hair was tied back this time—she had learned her lesson. And she was smiling at the baby and seemed happy—until she saw me. Then the smile and the rosy cheeks turned brick red as she glared at me. She was mad, and I was crushed. A second chance to be in the delivery room had just slipped away. She had every right to be furious. This was too big an event in our lives, and I should have stayed at the hospital and napped in a chair in the waiting room.

We named our second son Todd Joseph, and I promised once again to call both sets of parents. Before heading for the familiar pay phone, I gave both Todd and Barb a little kiss, hoping one of them would kiss back. But she didn't, and I wasn't surprised. With the sun coming up, I glumly returned home to reclaim Brian from the neighbors. I told him that he had a new baby brother who would be coming home with his mother in a few short days.

In midmorning, the telephone rang. It was Barb, and she had calmed a bit but really was more interested in talking to Brian than to me. Of course, like any three-year-old, Brian was on the phone and in tears in seconds.

"I miss you, Mommy," he wailed into the phone with his lower jaw quivering.

And I sensed there were just as many tears on the other end of the phone. A couple of hours later, I decided to take Brian down to Stewart Park to keep him occupied.

"Your Mommy and I were here watching these same deer, just before you were born."

"Will she be home today?" the now calm toddler asked.

"Not yet, but soon. And your new brother, Todd, will be there, too," I promised.

He played on the swings and we fed the ducks until it was time to head back to the apartment. I started to drive home and then on a whim turned the other way.

Even though it was now routine to allow fathers into the delivery room, it was still strictly forbidden to take children into hospitals for visits. At least I could drive Brian past the hospital to show him where his mother and new brother were staying. Tompkins County Hospital was a huge, old stone building, built during Cornell's early years. The architecture was similar to the older buildings on campus and almost identical to the dorm I had lived in only four years earlier. The building was set well back from the road, so I pulled into the parking lot to give Brian a better view.

"What room is Mommy in?" Brian inquired.

"Well, her room is on the other side of the building," I responded. "It's on the first floor in the far corner. Come on. Lets take a walk, and I'll show you her window."

The old building sat in a parklike setting on a bluff high above Cayuga Lake, across from the Cornell campus. It had sidewalks all the way around the building. So we walked hand in hand. The building had ancient leaded-glass windows that didn't open. The first floor windows were about six feet off the ground for privacy. When we reached the far back side of the building, it was easy to point out his mother's room. Incredibly, as I did, Barb appeared at the window, holding Todd. And somehow we all spotted each other.

Brian let out a shout, pulled away from my grip, and rushed over. He slipped through the hedges that surrounded the building. I crashed through an opening to try to retrieve him. I grabbed him, and as I stood inside of that row of hedges, there was just enough room to pick up Brian, and place him on my shoulders. Within seconds, he was laughing and banging lightly on the window. From my sharp angle on the ground, I could just make out Barb's face, blurred in the leaded-glass window. And I could tell she was showing him Todd under the blankets. And I could see the tears of joy and her rosy cheeks once again. They visited quietly for a few minutes, communicating with their hands until a nurse came into the room and ended the impromptu party.

It would be nice to say that the meeting in the bushes all happened because of some great planning on my part. But it wouldn't be true. It just happened. Sometimes it helps to be lucky. And because of the unexpected visit between Barbara and Brian, I stumbled onto a way that took most of the sting out of the fact that I had missed another delivery. And I was forgiven.

Chapter 9
Finding a Job
Buffalo, Spring 1976

IN THE SECOND HALF OF OUR FINAL year at Cornell, we all began looking for our first job as a veterinarian. The first year or two of employment have always been considered critical to a young vet's development. When the system works properly, a new graduate and an experienced animal doctor make a terrific combination. When difficult cases present themselves, both put their heads together to determine the best course of action. The mature vet, with years of experience handling similar cases, can generally determine the problem quicker than the neophyte. The newcomer, however, has more recent knowledge of new drugs and treatments that the practice owner may not have encountered. If neither allows ego to get in the way, the winners clearly are the sick pets and their owners.

Barb and I both hoped to return to Buffalo. We had started our family earlier than most, and we wanted our children to have a place they could call home as soon as possible. Economically, it was not a great time to return. Steel mills had been closing all over the Northeast. Other industries were beginning to move out of the area as well. As a very blue-collar city, the economic challenges for Buffalo were dramatic. Buffalo was in its worst shape since the Great Depression.

I had gone to the student placement office in the veterinary college to see what jobs were available in the Buffalo area. I found only three. One was from a practice in Orchard Park, perhaps the best-known practice in the Buffalo area. It was a hospital where other hospitals sent their most difficult cases for further workups. Unfortunately, it was marked, *Position Filled—January '76.* Of the other two, only one was recognizable. It was a well-respected practice in the downtown area, on Ellicott Street. The two brothers who operated it were both in their early sixties. Their father had started the practice before them at a time when veterinary medicine revolved around treating horses when the farmers brought their produce into town. Pictures depicting the long-since-relocated farmers' market hung on the reception room walls. Clearly, this practice had a respected history with Buffalo area pet owners and appeared to be the best position available in Buffalo. I made arrangements to interview there while home for the holidays.

Three days after Christmas, I went to the interview. One of the brothers greeted me and apologized that he had a minor surgery to perform before we could go to lunch. He invited me back to watch the surgery as he sutured up a laceration on the leg of a mixed-breed dog. We chatted as he worked. His brother was in the hospital, having just undergone cardiac bypass surgery. Their other associate, Dr. Alan, had recently committed twenty hours per week to the Buffalo Zoological Society. The society had recently replaced the city government as overseers of the zoo. All of that news excited me. I knew that getting a position as a zoo veterinarian was virtually impossible, as only the largest of zoos were able to retain a staff vet. Still, given my prior interest in wildlife science, I was interested in any possible exposure to zoo medicine. I indicated a willingness to volunteer a half day each week just for the opportunity to work with wildlife from around the world. The brother made a quick phone call to arrange for me to spend the next morning at the zoo with Dr. Alan.

I met Dr. Alan at a prearranged gate outside the zoo at daybreak. As we were introducing ourselves to each other, an animal handler pulled up in a jeep and asked us to check a llama that was having a difficult time delivering a calf. We both jumped into the jeep and sped away. It's a shame the public never experiences zoos at daybreak. Active animals scurried about at this hour as we drove along. We arrived to find that the llama had finally delivered her youngster. Dr Alan allowed me to help him check both out, and I gave mom injections to help the uterus contract and prevent infection. Once we were confident about the llamas, we drove to the newly completed veterinary hospital at the south end of the zoo.

It was interesting for me to see evidence of the many significant changes that the zoological society had made since taking over the zoo from the city. I remembered that, as youngster, one of the highlights of my zoo visits had been tossing marshmallows to the begging bears. Of course, years of a constant diet of marshmallows had left all of the bears with rotten teeth. There were photographs in the entrance of the hospital showing Dr. Alan and his personal dentist working on anesthetized bears. He stopped at the display and told me that each Sunday for several months they had worked on one bear at a time, performing root canal procedures with a Black & Decker drill until every bear was treated. Marshmallows were no longer available or allowed. Dr. Alan was proud of this accomplishment, and he radiated a love for the work he was doing at this zoo. I was impressed.

Dr. Alan invited me to assist first with a monkey that needed sedation and then with a giant tortoise that needed an examination and X-rays. When those tasks were accomplished, it was time to make some "house calls." The first stop was at the reptile house, where an alligator had undergone amputation of an infected leg. It was time for a postoperative checkup. Because the alligators in the pen were small, handling them was not a problem. However, when entering the large display, I nearly stepped on a nest of well-camouflaged eggs, then stumbled to avoid them. While no damage was done, the reptile house zookeeper seethed at this display of stupidity. Next, we treated a lizard with an eye infection. After that, Dr. Alan took me on a behind-the-scenes tour of the snake house. I was awed by the color-coded charts on the back of each cage that identified the appropriate antiserum for emergency use if anyone was bitten by a poisonous snake. It was both eerie and fascinating. Apparently, Marlin Perkins, who had been the curator of the Buffalo Zoo in his earlier days, had established the color-coding system many years earlier. Marlin later became famous for his *Wild Kingdom* television series. Our final house call of the morning was a visit to a seal with a neurological problem affecting its flippers. Nobody knew what was causing the rare problem. The seal was receiving multivitamin injections in hopes of reversing the nerve damage.

My incredible morning was over as my host needed to report downtown to the dog and cat hospital. The zoo had opened for the day, and visitors were beginning to wander around the park. Since I had not been at the zoo for several years, I meandered around for another hour. The morning's experience had changed my perspective. I found myself looking at the animals with a sense of watchfulness and concern rather than just with a sense of curiosity. These animals in pens and not in their natural environments needed care, and I imagined myself as one of their caretakers. I was no longer just a visitor at the zoo.

After the holidays, it was time for Barb and me to load the family into our rusty car and head back to Ithaca. I had every reason to hope that an offer would soon be forthcoming. In mid-January, Cornell hosted an annual conference where vets congregated for continuing education seminars and for interviewing graduating seniors. I went to the conference, and I was pleased to bump into the elderly brother from the Buffalo practice. He seemed genuinely pleased to see me, and he told me that I would be receiving an offer in the very near future. I thanked him and inquired how his brother was doing. Cardiac bypass was relatively new in those days. Fortunately, his brother was out of the hospital and making good progress at home.

The conference ended a few days later. I continued with school, expecting a job offer at any time. However, as the weeks went by, no contact occurred. I didn't want to seem pushy, and I continued my vigil. About two months after the conference, one of the professors inquired if I had lined up a position. I mentioned the practice I was hoping to join, and a puzzled look come over his face.

"I thought Larry accepted that job during the January conference," he said.

I was shocked. Larry probably had superior grades to mine, but as he was not from Western New York. I hadn't even known that he was interested in the job. Quality practices were typically choosy. They sought out the best students, and they hired them early on. I had no problem with the job being offered to a better student. However, I was stunned that there had been no contact or at the least a brief letter of regret from the Buffalo vets. As we were on different senior rotations, I hadn't crossed paths with Larry in a long time.

I tracked him down to confirm the news. He had no idea that I had applied for the job, and we both could only surmise that the downtown veterinarians believed I was aware of their decision.

Down but not out, the next day I went to the student placement office. I penciled *Position Filled* on the downtown job description and began to study the one opening at an unfamiliar Buffalo-area clinic in Depew. I recorded the name and telephone number and placed a call the next morning. The owner seemed pleased to hear from a senior. He explained that his associate of the past few years was leaving in a month or two to purchase a practice of his own. I had the following Friday free, so I set a date to drive home for a quick visit to the practice. At the prearranged time, I arrived at the practice to find an older but serviceable-looking clinic with no cars in the parking lot, which seemed strange for 10:30 on a Friday morning.

I entered the practice and introduced myself to the receptionist. Something seemed unusual, but I couldn't pinpoint the problem.

"Not very busy today?" I asked.

"The boss gave the vet that usually works on Friday the day off," she said. She seemed the outgoing type yet at the same time appeared to avoid eye contact.

"We only saw a few clients this morning," she said almost apologetically. "Doc is in the back working on a dog. He'll be right up." Once again something felt elusive about her demeanor.

The owner came from the back and introduced himself. We went to the treatment area and chatted as he finished up a minor surgery.

"The vet that is leaving soon asked for another day off," he grumped. I made a mental note of the discrepancy in the two stories, adding it to my uncertainty. Was there some reason why the owner didn't want me to meet the exiting associate?

After a tour of the hospital, we went down to the office in the basement to talk. I noticed that the office sported plush pink carpeting. After a short conversation, we left the clinic for lunch at a local eatery. During lunch, my host consumed three "virgin" cocktails to my one iced tea.

"Hey Doc, you're turning into a sissy! Can't handle the real stuff anymore?"

teased the waiter, who obviously knew this veterinarian well enough to joke about his choice of beverage. Again, I wondered. Might this guy be an alcoholic? Perhaps that was the missing piece of the puzzle. I remembered my experience at the poultry farm, and something inside of me said that this wasn't where I belonged.

During lunch, the clinic owner offered me the position at a thousand dollars over the going rate for new graduates. I felt a momentary temptation to accept the position, but my gut instinct simply wouldn't let me do it. I hedged my bets by telling him that I had other interviews scheduled, and I promised to give him a definite answer within two weeks. I knew that the other interviews didn't really exist, but I intended to set them up as soon as possible.

I drove back to Ithaca that evening to discuss the situation with Barbara. We were both undecided as to our next step. We dearly wanted to return home to Buffalo, and this position seemed to represent our last opportunity for that year. Our contingency plan was to try to find a position in Rochester, about ninety miles east of Buffalo. Rochester's economy was much stronger than Buffalo's. Rochester was a more white-collar community, with high-tech companies like Xerox and Kodak leading the way. A handful of good openings existed, and it was time for me to start interviewing there.

About four days later, I received an urgent telephone call from the owner of the Depew practice. Once again he was offering the job, even though the two weeks had not passed. I knew that I could not string this person along any further. I simply had to trust my best instincts that said it would be a major mistake to take that position. Taking a deep breath, I told him that I had decided against the position and wished him well. I gave no reason, as I did not want to burn any bridges that might be useful somewhere in the future.

The next day, I received a panicked call from my mother.

"You didn't take the job that you interviewed for last week, did you?" she asked nervously. "There was an article in today's paper about that vet. Apparently, he's under criminal investigation for sexual misconduct. The article hinted an employee was involved!"

I gasped as the thick pink carpeting in the office flashed through my mind, and I assured Mom that I had declined the position.

Once again, I headed for the student placement office. This time the focus would be on the Rochester job file. I picked up the folder, and I was about to open it when some mysterious force coerced me to pull the Buffalo file out of the cabinet one last time. I went through the Buffalo folder, hoping that some new opportunities would miraculously appear. There were no new jobs posted. I penciled *Watch Out* on the posting for the recently declined job, and I flipped through the rest of the cards. The file marked *Position filled—Jan. '76* stuck in my fingers.

Maybe, just maybe, things had not worked out there, and they were looking again, an inner voice suggested silently. Some gray matter rationalized that I should call this practice in Orchard Park before setting up interviews in Rochester.

I sped home at lunchtime to telephone the Orchard Park practice. The owners would probably not be in the building during the noon hour, but perhaps a receptionist could satisfy my curiosity. I inquired from the receptionist whether or not they were still interviewing for the staff veterinary position. She asked me to stay on hold for a moment as one of the owners was in the office. I was delighted when Dr. Jack picked up the telephone. He explained that the position was indeed filled, but he told me about the few opportunities nearby that might possibly be available. He told me about the downtown opening as well as the one I had just rejected.

"You will need to visit them and judge for yourself what kind of practices they represent," he suggested.

That statement was probably a veiled form of the *Watch Out* that I had just written on one file. I told him that I was familiar with those openings, but that things had not worked out with either for varying reasons. He took my name and number and promised to call me if he heard of any other openings or if he had any himself in the future. As he was wishing me well and was about to hang up, another idea came to his mind.

"Oh!" he said. "I just remembered. Have you called the practice down the road from us? The owner is Dr. Tom, and he took over a small older practice about a year and a half ago. He mentioned at a luncheon recently that he thought it might be time to consider an associate. It's a long shot if he's not yet advertising, but it might be worthwhile to touch base with him for future possibilities."

I was impressed that Dr. Jack had taken the time to get on the phone personally and discuss all this with me. It would have been much easier for him to have his receptionist tell me that their position was filled. I mentally noted that this was exactly how I wanted to deal with my fellow colleagues in the future.

I dialed the number that Dr. Jack had supplied and was pleased to hear that Dr. Tom was also in his office. We discussed the possibility of a position for a few minutes. He told me that the building itself was quite old but that he was in the early stages of designing a totally new hospital. I liked the optimism that I heard in Dr. Tom's voice. Barb and I were returning to Buffalo for a long Easter recess in ten days. He asked me to show up around ten in the morning on the Thursday before Easter for an on-site visit.

I had intended to use the spring break time wisely by calling a couple of the Rochester practices to set up a few appointments for Friday or Saturday. However, I didn't follow through on those intentions because I had a strange but strong confidence about this new possibility. Although it was true that Dr. Tom still had not made a definite commitment to hire an associate, I was beginning to listen harder to that little voice inside of me.

On the scheduled day, I arrived fifteen minutes early for the interview. My heart sank when I saw the building. I sat in my parked car for a few minutes and stared at the bleak buildings in front of me. There was an apparently vacant house next to the practice that was in great need of repairs or, better yet, demolition. The original owner of the practice had undoubtedly lived there sometime in the past. The practice building itself appeared to be an L-shaped building, coming out from what had probably been the original double garage for the house. Paint was peeling on many areas of the building, creating an unsightly first impression.

I took a deep breath and entered the waiting room. Suddenly my mood shifted for the better. The interior of the building seemed bright and much more presentable.

"Hi, I'm Eleanor," announced a very friendly receptionist. "You must be the senior veterinary student we've been looking forward to meeting. Have a seat, we'll be with you in a jiffy!"

Moments later a friendly technician came out to introduce herself to me.

"Hi, I'm Sheila, one of the technicians," she said. "Follow me and I'll introduce you to Dr. Tom. Then we'll both give you a tour."

Despite the worn outside of the building, I was instantly impressed with these two warm and friendly greeters. And it took only moments to feel the sense of pride that Dr. Tom had in his efforts to transform, at midcareer, from a large animal practitioner to a small animal specialist. As we toured the facility, he pointed with pride to the brand new X-ray machine, adding that the radiology company had promised to move it to the new location free of charge when the new hospital was ready. He pointed out how the old one-table surgery room had recently been converted into a second examination room. This allowed the conversion of a former kennel area into a double-table surgery. He told me how he had been attending many seminars and visiting other veterinarians in his effort to learn the latest advances in small animal surgery. He spoke of how wonderful it would be to have a new graduate on the staff to discuss recent developments in surgery and all the new medications that were becoming available. We both sensed that we were comfortable with each other from the start.

Over lunch, Dr. Tom tentatively offered me the position and asked that I bring Barb to his home on Friday evening. That meeting went without a hitch. The spouses met each other, and Dr. Tom presented us with a letter of agreement stating the terms of employment. Starting salary would be the typical $17,500 per year with full family health insurance provided.

Finally, my tortuous adventure to land a job after graduation had come to an end. The emotional cycles of first excitement and then disappointment were behind us. With a job firmly in hand, all we needed to do was to find an apartment in the neighborhood and prepare to move in two months. We quickly found a newly built duplex near the clinic, and we signed a lease on Easter Sunday.

Returning to Ithaca, all that remained was another six weeks of clinical rotation, graduation day, and a grueling two-day licensing exam. In no time at all, we were gathered around a graduation cake designed by Barb, with both sets of parents visiting on commencement day. Several days later the exam was complete, the rented truck was loaded, and we were ready to shuffle off to Buffalo.

Suddenly something was bleating loudly in the background. I realized the alarm clock was trying its best to tell me it was morning. Without much sleep, it was time to get up and head to the clinic to make certain Patti, the dog whose bladder I had nicked accidentally, was doing well.

Chapter 10
Dr. Tom's First Vacation
West Seneca, July 1976

EVERYTHING WAS FINE IN THE HOSPITAL that morning. Patti went home without any problems, and the technicians clearly appreciated the fact that I had accepted all the blame. But my life dragged forward slowly, with my confidence badly shaken.

The next two weeks at the animal hospital seemed like torture. Rather than settling into a new job, I was depressed going to work each day and dreaded dealing with each and every client. Practice was nothing like I had envisioned, and what started out a month earlier as a healthy fear of failure was slowly but steadily morphing to a full-blown realization of failure.

One afternoon, a client arrived with a cat that had been ill for days and had died en route to the hospital. I entered the exam room to confirm that it was dead. There was no heartbeat, and all eye reflexes were gone. The pet owners were distraught and feeling guilty for not seeking medical care sooner. Like most anyone stunned by an unexpected loss, they asked if I had any idea what had gone wrong. I looked at the medical records, noticing the cat was twelve years old. As I handled the body, I could feel a large mass in the abdomen.

"I can feel a tumor. It was cancer no doubt," I said confidently. "We would not have been able to offer any treatment."

As I carried the body to the back of the hospital, I felt the abdomen again. This time I realized that the mass was a round smooth structure. I placed the body on a table and checked to see if it was male or female—I simply had not looked at the medical records closely enough. Indeed it was a male cat, and instantly I knew this was case of urinary obstruction. The mass I was feeling was actually a grossly distended bladder, often referred to as a "plugged tomcat." It was an unusual finding in a cat this age but certainly not impossible. Had the owners sought medical attention sooner, it would have been treatable. The wrong information I'd given the owners probably helped them through a difficult time, but I was devastated by my absurd misdiagnosis. What if the cat had still been alive? Might I have euthanized a treatable patient out of ignorance? Any third-year veterinary student would have recognized the situation, but I had blown it.

At that moment, I decided it was best to plan for an alternative career. I knew where the dreaded boneyard for veterinarians awaited; those who could not make the transition to clinical practice often ended up working for the USDA as meat inspectors. It was mindless work, inspecting carcasses of animals in a slaughterhouse. Oh well, I mused. At least it was steady work that would allow me to support the family I was about to let down. It was a gruesome thought, but having alternative plans in life had served me well as a student, and now it was time to do the same for my career.

To make matters worse, Dr. Tom was heading out of town soon for a week of vacation with his family. It was July, and the heat outside meant we would be extremely busy in the practice. Dog and cat illnesses peak during the summer, and the incidence of skin problems soar. Without question, I wasn't remotely ready for the challenge.

Monday, the first day of Dr. Tom's vacation, was particularly long. We saw patients until noon, and then we had a long break, followed by appointments late into the afternoon and evening. Fortunately, I had received permission from Dr. Tom to move a better light into the new surgery room. The increased illumination helped, but I still was struggling to see fine detail during surgery. I had decided to take advantage of the long break on Monday and scheduled an appointment with an ophthalmologist down the road from the practice. Despite all my medical knowledge, I was taken by surprise when the doctor used drops to dilate my pupils for the exam. Previously, an optician rather than an ophthalmologist had examined me, and my eyes were not dilated.

"Don't worry," said the nurse, "Most people's pupils return to normal within an hour or so, and we have disposable sunglasses for you to wear."

Unfortunately, I soon discovered that I did not fit into the category of "most" people. My eyes were hypersensitive to the drops, and my pupils dilated dramatically. Just driving back to the office was a nightmare. Having grown up in Western New York, I was experienced driving in snowstorms even with whiteout conditions, but this was worse. Despite the sunglasses and the visor down in the car, I could barely see the lines on the highway. Other vehicles slithered by in blurry, ghostlike fashion. Thankfully, the drive was short, and somehow I made it back to the practice without incident.

Inside, I darkened both exam rooms, turning out lights and closing the blinds. Then I summoned Sheila and Paula to formulate a plan.

"They said my pupils will be back to normal very soon. So I don't think we should cancel appointments. You two may need to be my eyes for the first few appointments, but after that everything should be OK."

Sheila and Paula agreed. There must have been something intriguing about working with me, and they accepted the challenge. Unfortunately, my pupils remained dilated for what seemed like forever. I had to examine all of the animals in semidarkened exam rooms for the next few hours. I can only guess what the pet owners must have been thinking.

Since it was midsummer, part of each examination was to check closely for fleas. I would pick up a flea comb, pull it through the pet's fur, and hand it to Sheila or Paula to examine. Giving advice on how to treat flea problems was one thing I could do with my eyes closed or, in this case, too wide open. Giving vaccinations was a whole different challenge. I could see the pets, but not with any sharpness or clarity. I felt like I was practicing veterinary medicine by Braille.

Thankfully, as afternoon transitioned to evening, my pupils finally returned to normal, and I finished off the remainder of the appointments with clear vision. I finished the day exhausted and frustrated. Even though the staff and I had found a way to make everything work, I couldn't believe that I, with all of my medical training, had failed to anticipate how an eye exam would go. It was yet another sign that veterinary medicine wasn't where I belonged.

If Monday was bad, Tuesday was a nightmare. We had a full load of surgery scheduled in the morning. While covering emergencies overnight, I had admitted an older dog with a pyometra—a severe and life-threatening infection of the uterus. I knew how urgent it was to perform a complete hysterectomy as soon as possible. The bacteria that cause the infection secrete a toxin that could shut down kidney function. This was one surgical procedure that should never be delayed. The veterinary school mantra of "never let the sun rise or set on a pyometra" played in my head. I had already violated that rule, as there was no way to do this complicated surgery alone in the middle of the night. I told the techs that we would do this surgery first, keenly aware that the sun had already risen on this pet.

The procedure took almost two hours. The uterus, which would generally be the diameter of a pencil, was filled with pus and swollen to the size of a thick sausage. On top of that, the dog was obese, and the toxicity of the infection had caused some of the internal body fat to break down. Everything inside the abdomen had an oily coating. Handling the uterus was like handling a greased pig, only worse. If I tugged or pulled too hard and the uterus ruptured in my hands, the dog would likely die of peritonitis—an abdominal infection. I successfully finished the surgery, but by the end of it, I was absolutely exhausted. Having admitted the pet in the middle of the night, I hadn't gotten much sleep. And yet a full slate of surgeries awaited that were scheduled to be completed by one o'clock, when afternoon appointments began.

Somehow we sloughed through the remaining surgeries. The last one came off the table a few minutes before two o'clock. There would be no lunch for any of us again as we were already late starting afternoon appointments. The waiting room was full.

It seemed as though every pet south of Buffalo was ill that day, and six impatient clients were already in the waiting room with pets suffering from various ailments. As we dragged though the afternoon appointments, all the clients seemed on edge, both worried about their pets and annoyed by the wait. The last appointment was scheduled at five o'clock, although the office did not officially close until six. On most days we finished the last appointment comfortably by six. On this day, the last client walked out the door at ten past seven.

As the employees scurried out the door, already late for their evening commitments, I sat in the office and closed my eyes, exhausted physically, and destroyed mentally. How had I managed to get through the rigors of vet school? I had handled the student load and had even worked part-time the first three years. There were occasions when I had worked all night on the chicken farm, helping the state veterinarian blood-test thousands of birds. We had screened incoming chickens for salmonella infection before they would be released into the pens. I'd been able to work through the night, scoot home, shower, and head to campus for a full day of academics. Why was I feeling so inept now?

On Wednesday morning, things finally seemed to settle down. I handled all of the scheduled appointments, and the dog recovering from pyometra surgery was doing fine. Then around ten o'clock, Eleanor, our receptionist and office manager interrupted.

"Doc, sorry to bother you, but there's a phone call that you need to take."

I was stunned. Eleanor never interrupted either Dr. Tom or me in the middle of an office call. I excused myself and headed for the phone. What could it be? Had something happened to Barb? The boys? Or perhaps my parents?

"Hi Doc," retorted a friendly voice on the other end of the phone. "This is Steve, down at the main post office on Dingens Street. George just brought in an envelope that he found in the mailbox next to the Marine Midland bank that's near your office. The envelope appears to be a thick bank deposit envelope, and it has your animal clinic's name on the front."

My jaw dropped. One of the duties I had inherited during Dr. Tom's vacation was to take the mail and the bank deposit over to the bank each night, depositing each in their appropriate slot.

"Oh no!" I exclaimed. "That's my fault. I must have put it in the mailbox by error last night. I can't believe I did something that stupid."

"Don't worry, Doc!" Steve chuckled. "You're not the first one. We've been telling management for years that mailboxes shouldn't be placed near bank night-deposit slots, but no one listens to us. I wish I could send this envelope to your office with your route carrier, but I'm not allowed to do that. Someone from your office needs to come downtown between eight and four to identify the envelope and sign for it."

"I'll be there as soon as possible on my lunch hour today," I reassured. "Thanks so much for calling. I feel like such a fool."

A couple of hours later, I drove downtown as fast as possible. By the time I arrived, Steve was back from his lunch break. He took me in the back and had me sign for the envelope.

"Don't feel so bad," he said with a grin. "This happens a couple of times each week somewhere in the city. Most of them are personal deposits, not thick business deposits like this one. Fortunately, John, who picks up mail on that route, is as honest as they come. You'll be laughing about this in a few days."

For whatever reason, Steve liked me and sensed how devastated I felt.

"Come over here a second, Doc. I want to show you something," he added.

He took a key from his desk drawer and walked over to a locked filing cabinet.

"We find all sorts of things. Some make sense, like a child's toy or even a small book. But take a look at this beauty," he said as he pulled out a small envelope and removed a sparkling engagement ring with an enormous stone.

"My brother's a jeweler," he said holding the glistening gem up for better lighting. "I had him stop by and look at this beauty a long time ago. It's the real deal, probably about two carats! It's been in this drawer for almost a year now. No one has shown up to claim it. It's scheduled to go to auction soon. Your story is funny, Doc, but I bet if this ring could talk we'd hear one hell of a spicier tale!"

Amazed, I agreed with Steve and headed back to the office. It was helpful that he had tried to make me feel better, but medical professionals were expected to be above stupid errors, and mine was as absentminded as could be.

Somehow I dragged through the rest of the week. I couldn't wait for Dr. Tom to return. There was no way I would ever be able to run a practice on my own.

CHAPTER 11

Smokey
West Seneca, August 1976

WITH DR. TOM BACK IN TOWN, the nightmare of running the practice alone was gone, but the next challenge didn't take long to arrive. Our own ten-year-old beagle, Smokey, became very ill a few days later. He was one of a litter of six pups born in our home during my junior year of high school, and he was the last of the beagles that I would raise during my high school years. Smokey wasn't just the last of a line. He was symbolic to me in many ways.

First, he and his littermates were destined to be hunting dogs, so in some small way he represented my love for the outdoors and my original goal to pursue a career in wildlife science. But, more importantly, he represented a time when I knew very little about veterinary medicine and, for that matter, not quite enough about animal husbandry. We had bred his mother, Tina, with a beagle owned by a high school classmate, and we all had waited for the puppies to arrive. I read up on whelping and thought I was ready. With Dad's help, we built a whelping box in the basement.

When Tina finally went into labor, we doted over her endlessly. I had no clue that dogs do a fine job of controlling their own labor and are even able to delay labor if they cannot find solitude. We unwittingly stressed Tina to no end hovering over her. Despite our interference, she managed to produce three healthy pups. I had hoped for a larger litter, but I went to bed satisfied that everything had gone well.

In the morning, I sprang down the basement steps to see how things were going, and I was stunned to see six wiggling, cooing pups nosily nursing away. One of the new pups was different from the others. Rather than being the typical tricolored beagle—black with white and brown markings—his black areas were mostly grey. He quickly became the family favorite, and he earned the name Smokey. Little did I realize that his colors were likely to change, and by the time he was four months old, he looked just like the rest of his littermates. There wasn't a hint of grey remaining in his coat. During my years in vet school, his name or, more appropriately, his misnomer, stood as a constant reminder of how much I had to learn and later how far I had come.

Smokey became the family pet, living with my parents and younger brother during the years that I was at school in Ithaca. Thanks in part to my regular returns to Buffalo, I saw him often. And despite my absence, he was always my dog. By the time I was in vet school, he was showing signs of aging. He stayed with us in Ithaca on two brief occasions, and both times, he was used as a teaching case. He had developed eyelid growths, so he underwent two different surgical procedures under the care of the ophthalmology service. But now, years later, he was developing much more serious problems. He was clearly in extreme pain, and the diagnosis was a herniated cervical disc—a ruptured spinal disc in his neck. It's a condition seen more often in beagles than in other breeds. And the pain in some cases is excruciating.

I started out treating Smokey with the limited medications of the '70s—mostly anti-inflammatory medications. It helped in some cases and did not in others. It did not help Smokey. His episodes of acute pain were getting worse, so we moved him from my parent's house, north of the city, to our home. I wanted to monitor him closely and relieve my parents of the strain and heartache of it all. Finally, with his condition deteriorating and the pain almost constant, I took him to surgery. However, as with all spinal surgery, it sometimes worked and sometimes did not. Even when specialists at the university level perform these surgeries, only some of the cases respond.

For three days after surgery, Smokey seemed to do well. There were even brief moments when the old Smokey seemed to reappear. I warned Barb and my parents that things could get worse at any time. The disc could herniate further, or any of the other discs in the neck could rupture as well. On day five, his pain was back as bad as ever. Then came day six. That Saturday night, he slept on blankets and pillows in the kitchen because going up the stairs to our second-floor bedroom was clearly too painful. On Sunday morning, his sixth day post-op, he was nowhere to be found. We called his name with no response. He had to be somewhere. Finally, Barb found him behind the couch. He had somehow wedged himself tightly between the couch and the wall. His eyes blinked, and his breathing was heavy. But other than that, he lay motionless and silent. We moved the couch and carried him back to the kitchen. A quick examination revealed my worst fears. Both front legs were paralyzed with no pain perception. We waited a few hours to make sure the signs were not temporary from being pinned behind the couch, but I knew from the start it was not the cause of his symptoms. I knew that he was in so much pain that he had simply stopped trying. And the look in his eyes said it all. He was begging for relief from the pain he was trying to hide.

Barb and I made the difficult decision that it was time to put him down to relieve his suffering.

"You'll need help. I'll get the boys ready, and we can go to the office with you," Barb said.

"Thanks, but there is no way I want a five-year-old to witness the execution of his first and only pet, no matter how appropriate it might be," I responded. "Don't worry, I can handle it alone," I told her with a hug, struggling to hold back tears. In my heart, I knew this was personal—between Smokey and me. I simply had to do it myself.

I loaded him into the car and drove to the hospital. Every time I moved him, I could feel him tense with excruciating pain. But he never moved. I laid him on the floor in an exam room, fearful he might fall from a table. But he never moved. Once everything was ready, I lifted him to the table and placed a tourniquet around his leg. As much as I wanted to delay the next step, I knew I had to work quickly before emotion made it hard for me to find a vein.

Luckily the needle found its target on the first try. Releasing the tourniquet, I slowly injected the solution. As I did, I could feel his body relax. We exchanged one last glance, he blinked one last time, but he never moved. His pain was gone. And so was he.

"Take care buddy," I mumbled with moistened eyes as I caressed his head.

I slumped onto the bench where clients generally sat, tears rolling down my face. I was upset, with the emotions of loss anyone would have felt. I did feel some small sense of relief, knowing that I had managed the procedure without any struggle or delay. I took some comfort in knowing that I was able to once and forever stop the pain.

But mostly I felt like a failure. I had not been able to save or cure Smokey, and I blamed myself for that. Should I have tried other medications? Should I have taken him back to Cornell to be examined by the specialists?

In the end I felt that my inability to help him was the loudest and clearest symbol of all. It was an obvious sign of my failure as a veterinarian, and it indicated that it was time to move on. Every ounce of Smokey's lifeless body on the table told me, loud and clear, that my clinical career was every bit as dead.

I sat there at least ten minutes staring off into space. Finally, I moved his body to the morgue and cleaned the exam room. This was one time I needed to make certain that Sheila or Paula did not have to clean up my mess. Only I should do that now.

I started for the door and then hesitated for a moment. I needed to telephone my parents and let them know Smokey was gone. And I didn't want to make that call from home. I went to the business office and sat down by a telephone. I slowly dialed the familiar number. My mother answered the phone, and immediately I lost all control of my emotions. I cried in a way she hadn't heard since I was ten years old. It took at least a minute to work in that Smokey was gone—in garbled words interspersed between uncontrolled sobs. I was twenty-five miles from home, but I could feel my mother's shock on the other end of the line. She assumed that I was overly upset about Smokey, and at some level that was true. But it was so much more than that. It was my sense of failure. It was my feeling guilty for not having discussed these feelings with Barb, much less with my parents. And I couldn't tell Mom any of that for the moment. Barb deserved to be the first to hear my words. I would tell her that I was not fit to be a clinical veterinarian.

The inability to control my emotions was more evidence of my failure. I was supposed to be a professional, with the ability to help and comfort others at a time like this. I was not a good veterinarian at all. I was a person who had just made Smokey's loss all the more difficult for my parents. And it was because of my guilt. There was no excuse for that.

I drove home, and within minutes, my whole family was crying. Barb and the boys were crying for Smokey, and I was crying because the world was crashing down around me, and I couldn't find a way to warn any of them. Smokey was a great dog and was headed for better places. I was stuck in my own private hell.

We went out for dinner that evening, trying to pretend that everything was normal. Kids are resilient. The boys were already on to other thoughts and dreams. But Barb and I were silent. In general, Barb was more emotional about pets while I was more pragmatic. Her silence was probably about Smokey, but perhaps not. Was she making the same wrong assumptions about me that I was sure my mother was making? Or did she sense what I was going through? How would she react when I finally told her what was happening? And my feelings of inadequacy and guilt grew and grew.

That evening, while Barb was upstairs putting the boys to bed, I went to the desk, pulled out some stationery, grabbed a veterinary journal, and found the ever-present classified ad for meat inspectors. I quickly handwrote a note to the USDA, requesting an application. After stuffing and stamping the envelope, I went to the car and put it in the glove compartment. I would find a way to tell Barb about all this, but not today. She was still upset about Smokey, and I could use that excuse to delay any conversation a day or two longer. But I knew it was wrong.

CHAPTER 12
Squeaky
West Seneca, September 1976

FOR THE NEXT FEW DAYS, A NIGHTMARE haunted my sleep. I was in a grocery store with Barb and our sons. Barb was looking at steaks in the cooler in the meat department. Brian was holding her hand, trying his best to stand on his toes to peek over the top into the cooler to see what his mother was doing. Todd, our two-year-old, was sound asleep in the grocery cart that I was pushing. Behind the counter, several butchers were cutting and trimming meat. One side of beef hung from a hook behind the work area. On the beef were several of the well-known purplish blue stamps placed there by federal meat inspectors. I knew government veterinarians working to protect our meat supply had affixed those stamps. The stamps were supposed to say USDA, but these were different. They were more like purple eyeballs. They seemed to follow us as we walked down the aisle. They were staring at me and watching my family. Then I jerked awake, terrified and in a cold sweat.

The next morning, I arrived at the office a few minutes early. I knew there would be plenty of shock as well as sympathy about Smokey since his condition had turned for the worse so rapidly. I recounted the story of his decline to Sheila and Paula and accepted their condolences. At long last, I made it through some part of the process with a degree of professional decorum. No tears, although everyone recognized I was depressed, and they assumed they knew the reason. I knew at some point it would be necessary to sit down privately with Dr. Tom to discuss the future. I had committed to a one-year contract and was prepared to see it through. Yet at the same time,

71

I knew that snowflakes would be flying soon and business would slow for the winter. If Dr. Tom was as frustrated with the situation as I, perhaps this could end more quickly. Once I scheduled a meeting with him, I knew that I would have to break all this to Barb and to deal with the consequences and the realities of the future. However, today a built-in excuse to procrastinate at least one more day became available. Dr. Tom was attending a seminar in the afternoon, so he would only be in the building until noon.

Just before I entered the exam room for the final office call of the morning, Eleanor called me aside. She wanted to warn me about the case in Exam 2. It was a young single mother and her daughter with a pathetic looking twelve-week-old kitten. She wanted me to know that Miss Kimble had very little money, that she believed that the kitten needed to be euthanized, but that she was concerned about how her daughter would react. I entered the room, exchanging glances with Miss Kimble who seemed about the same age as Barb and I. Then I looked at the daughter, a skinny, teary-eyed child roughly the same age as Brian. Clutched tightly in her arms was the pathetic looking kitten—thin as a rail, except for the belly that was grotesquely distended. I knew instantly this was likely a case of FIP—feline infectious peritonitis. It's a disease that could show up in many forms. The worst form was called the wet form, and it was typically fatal. It occurred in young kittens and caused tremendous amounts of fluid to accumulate in the abdomen. I knew immediately that Miss Kimble was right, and right away I thought about how I had shielded Brian from the trauma of euthanizing Smokey just twenty-four hours earlier.

One of the things I'd discovered in my short career was that parents seemed to appreciate it if I talked to the child or children first; asking them questions as I gleaned needed information. If the child was self-assured enough to answer the questions, the parents were proud and simply filled in the blanks of the story. If the child was shy, the parents would take over and the child would withdraw and hide her head in mommy or daddy's clothing. Either way, the adults seemed to appreciate my efforts. I expected this little girl would fit the second category, but I decided to give it a try. I bent down on one knee to be at her level.

"Hi there. What's your kitty's name?" I asked.

"Squeaky," volunteered the little girl in a squeaky voice.

"That's a cool name," I responded. "Squeaky looks like she's pretty sick. Can I take a look at her?"

To my amazement, the skinny little arms that were wrapped around the kitten slowly unraveled and pushed the kitten toward me. Glancing up at her mother, I slowly stood up and laid Squeaky on the exam table. A brief exam revealed almost everything I had expected. The kitten was gaunt. Her eyes were sunken in. They told me she had given up. The abdomen felt turgid rather than squishy, more so than I had expected. In short, there was a pathetic two-pound kitten on the table, barely moving, with an abdomen distended to the size of a tennis ball and stretched just as tightly. It was obvious that Squeaky was close to death.

After another glance at Miss Kimble, I turned back toward the little girl.

"I need to run some tests on Squeaky to see what's wrong," I said. "Why don't you take your mommy home, and I'll call her in a little bit to decide what's best for Squeaky?" I was amazed when she took her mother's hand and headed for the door. Miss Kimble seemed even more shocked and thanked me with her eyes. "I'll phone you within an hour," I said directing my voice to the adult.

I carried Squeaky toward the back of the hospital with every intention of placing her in a cage where she would await the phone call that would give me official clearance to end her suffering. As I walked past the X-ray room, the taut feel of the kitten's abdomen haunted me one more time. Paula was walking by, so I asked her to snap a quick X-ray. It was obvious that she felt it was a strange request, but she exposed a film plate without comment. I sat down on the X-ray table with Squeaky lying next to me and waited for the test results. Dr. Tom passed by on his way out the door. He glanced at the kitten.

"An obvious case of FIP, and Eleanor says the owner has no money. Cut your losses and euthanize that kitten," he advised. "You probably should have sent them to the SPCA to save them even more money."

"I know, Tom. I'll handle it," I responded quietly. "Thanks."

Just as the outside door closed behind our boss, Paula reappeared with the X-ray and clipped it to the viewer. The abdomen contained plenty of fluid, to be sure, but it was different than I had expected. Rather than being spread throughout the abdomen, making the intestines hard to visualize, it appeared to be confined to one round ball filling the center of most of the abdomen. It was as though the tennis ball I felt was staring at me. Bells and whistles should have gone off in my head. But they didn't. I was simply perplexed.

As I walked to the office to telephone Miss Kimble, something continued to haunt me about the X-ray, and I formulated a plan. On the phone, I described FIP and how it affects young cats.

"But something really bothers me about the X-ray," I added. "I'm probably wrong, and it's probably FIP, but I'd like to find out what's going on. I'd like to take Squeaky to surgery to give her every last chance."

"Thanks, Doc. I really appreciate how you handled my daughter. But I can't possibly afford surgery. I need to put her down."

"I know. But I'd still like to take a peek," I responded. "I've never done this before, but I'll cover the cost of the surgery. Squeaky will likely die on the table. It will be better for your daughter that way, and we will have given Squeaky every possible chance."

Miss Kimble thanked me and gave me permission to proceed. It was a diabolical plan and a stupid decision. The likelihood of finding something repairable seemed close to zero. Our family budget was tight, although I knew there was a tiny bit of room. My student loan payments hadn't kicked in quite yet. But mostly it was my insane chance to be defiant. I had unintentionally screwed up numerous things in my first four months in practice. It was time to screw up on purpose. Dr. Tom would be furious, but it would make it easier to sit down with him to discuss the future. And that would force me to come clean with everyone else, starting with Barbara. I had a tiny belief that something weird was going on with this kitten, and I so wanted to protect a pitiful four-year-old girl. At the same time, I knew full well that I was using the situation for my own purposes. And I wasn't proud of that.

Common sense would have told any veterinarian to do an abdominal tap, to carefully insert a needle into the abdomen and withdraw a sample of the fluid. The color and consistency could help determine the problem. Also, examining it under a microscope to observe the cells and makeup of the fluid could help. But I was well beyond any notion of common sense. I saw my opening, and I was determined to take it.

"Prep Squeaky for surgery," I ordered. "I'm going in to see if we can figure out why this X-ray looks so weird."

Paula and Sheila just looked at each other.

"Now? During lunch?" one of them finally said, hoping to bring me to my senses.

"Yep," I responded with conviction. "It's the only time we have today, and she's not going to last much longer."

They didn't quite know how to respond. They knew I deserved a bit of leeway, having euthanized my own pet recently, but they also knew how Dr. Tom would feel. They saw that there may well be a train wreck ahead that I didn't see. They had no inkling that I had already decided to step in front of that train.

From our earlier escapades, Paula and Sheila had just enough faith in me to follow the order. Twenty minutes later, Squeaky was under anesthesia, laid out on her back with her grossly distended abdomen pointed skyward.

In those days, esophageal stethoscopes were used to monitor the depth of anesthesia. It's a small tube passed partway down the esophagus until the tip is at the level of the heart. A small cylindrical stethoscope on the end of the tube transmitted the sound of the heartbeats back to a small box with a speaker. On most cats and dogs, this provided the sounds of a heartbeat with a sound similar to what one would hear with a traditional stethoscope. However, when we inserted the stethoscope into Squeaky's esophagus, rather than a typical heartbeat, we heard a thin, rapid heartbeat that was "squeaky" in every sense of the word. As I placed drapes around the area of the incision, I realized for the first time how thinly her abdominal skin was stretched over the bulge. It was tissue-paper thin and so transparent that I could see many small blood vessels underneath, weaving back and forth over the area. Thanks to new eyeglasses, I could just make out tiny pulsations in some of the bigger vessels vibrating in total harmony with the sounds coming from the speaker.

For the initial incision, I raised a scalpel and drew the lightest line possible down the center of the abdomen. It parted like the Red Sea, exposing the muscle layer below. There was absolutely no body fat to be found. If the tissue-paper skin had been almost transparent, the stretched muscle layer below was almost translucent. I could easily see the line separating the major abdominal muscles. Once again, with as gentle a touch as possible, I feathered the scalpel over that line. The muscle layers parted in a similar manner. A smooth glistening layer was trying to push up through the opening. Having learned important lessons on my first day of surgery, I laid down the scalpel and probed the edges of the surface with my smallest finger. It wasn't peritoneum—the lining of the abdomen—and it wasn't attached to the bottom of the muscle layers. Could it be bladder like my first day in surgery? I glanced over the top rim of my new and unfamiliar glasses, and I saw Sheila watching with a sense of bewilderment.

"Has this cat passed any urine?" I queried.

"Yes, she was urinating in the cage just before we started anesthesia," assured Sheila.

"Good, then this probably isn't bladder," I muttered. "Grab a sterile syringe and needles. Let's tap it and see what comes out." I was finally ready to do what I should have done an hour earlier. As I drew back on the syringe, a fluid came out that seemed a bit like urine, only darker. "I don't think this is FIP. That fluid is always thick and full of fibrin clots." I emptied the full syringe into a pan and drew out another. It was when I emptied the syringe for the fourth time that a small lightbulb flickered in the back of my mind. "Hydronephrosis?" I mumbled to myself under my breath.

"Hyrdo *what*?" asked Sheila.

"Hydronephrosis," I repeated louder and with some conviction. As I continued to drain syringe after syringe from the slowly deflating tennis ball, I switched to lecture mode, trying to parrot to Sheila and Paula what I could remember from a junior year surgery lecture two years earlier.

"It's an extremely rare condition. Urine normally forms in the tubes of the kidney and is collected in a funnellike area in the center, called the renal pelvis. Normally it drains from the kidney to the bladder through the ureter.

If something happens to stop the flow of urine, pressure backs up in the affected kidney, destroying the tissue and turning it into a useless balloon full of liquid. It is very rare," I said as I tried to visualize the surgical scene from different angles.

"In fact, the most common way for it to happen is for a surgeon to accidentally tie off one of the ureters during a spay," I added to Sheila and Paula and perhaps to myself, being certain to finish the entire lecture, including the warning intended to scare young surgeons.

"Is there anything you can do?" Sheila asked.

"Well, in theory, if the other kidney is fine, this kidney could be removed to solve the problem. *But,* it's a major procedure, and this kitten is fading rapidly," I warned. "We've got nothing to lose. I'm going to clamp it off blindly and get it out of here as quickly as possible. I'll just hope for the best."

While I talked, I was feeling around the now-deflated globe, checking out the other kidney. It felt normal. Then I grabbed a curved hemostat, reached blindly under the base of the useless kidney, and clamped it off.

"If I catch any other important tissue, like the other ureter or a major blood vessel, the kitten won't have a chance," I predicted.

I was already looping a piece of absorbable suture around the stump below the hemostat, drawing a surgeon's knot tightly without being able to see how things were going. I looped a second piece of suture in the same area and blindly secured another knot. Next I took a second curved hemostat and clamped off the neck of the kidney just above the first hemostat. Finally, I took a deep breath, grabbed a curved pair of scissors, and made a cut between the two hemostats. The useless organ that was once a kidney broke loose and virtually floated to the top of the surgical field. I pulled it gently through the opening in the muscle layers, coaxing it outside the kitten's body. I turned it over to assess any damage. There was some extra tissue attached, and I stared at it carefully shifting my head from side to side, hoping the new glasses would magnify it even more.

"She's a small kitten, so it's hard to tell," I said. "But I'm pretty sure this is one of her ovaries. Good. That shouldn't matter."

Squeaky's pulse was growing slower and weaker. I started to suture the abdominal muscles and skin back together as fast as possible, trying not to tear the paper-thin layers.

"Turn off the gas anesthesia and let her start to wake up," I directed. "Be ready. If she starts to wake up, we can turn it back on."

But Squeaky never stirred as I sutured. We placed her in a cage and watched her lie there the rest of the day—breathing away but never regaining consciousness. There was little we could do but wait, and I told everyone, including Miss Kimble, that I didn't expect her to live. It all was just too much for her tiny system. But at least we had made the right decision and did what we could.

As I left the building for the night, nothing had changed. Squeaky would no doubt die quietly during the night. And it would be over. I drove home exhausted, totally forgetting about the letter to the USDA until I was home. I glanced at the glove compartment and then decided to mail it tomorrow, right after the train wreck.

Chapter 13
Nine Lives
West Seneca, September 1976

THAT NIGHT AS I TRIED TO SLEEP, a strange sense of calm descended. I was certain Squeaky would expire peacefully during the night, and I understood that some part of my career would expire as well. I was ready for that. I decided not to return to the hospital that night as I had in the past.

I walked into the hospital the next morning ready for anything. Or so I thought. Sheila was the first person to walk past me. There was a devilish twinkle in her eyes.

"Squeaky's eating!" she whispered loud enough for me to hear but quietly enough to be certain that Dr. Tom could not.

My worst fear was that Squeaky would still be alive but unconscious, so to hear that she was conscious *and* hungry seemed too good to be true. I headed straight for the kennel room. Paula was standing in front of the open cage door with a can of cat food in one hand and a tongue depressor in the other. Squeaky was standing up and ravenously licking morsels of canned food from the end of the tongue depressor.

"Easy, Paula," I cautioned. "Not too much! If she eats too much too fast, it could do more harm than good. Give her no more than a tablespoon or so every two hours until she moves her bowels, if she gets that far. Same with the water."

"OK, Doc. You got it," Paula responded with a gleam of pride in her eyes. "Cats really do have nine lives, don't they?"

I hadn't thought about it that way, but I had to admit she had a point.

However, I didn't want to get overly excited, and I hadn't lost sight of the fact that I'd broken a lot of rules to get this far.

"Yep. But she's not out of the woods by any means," I warned. "That other kidney could fail, or any number of other complications could set in."

But Squeaky's eyes weren't listening to me. She was still a skinny, pathetic runt of a kitten, but her eyes were alive and no longer sunken into her head. I headed to the phone, called Miss Kimble, and repeated all the warnings.

The biggest problem we had that day was Squeaky's constant meowing from the kennel area. She was clearly screaming for more food. Dr. Tom never said a word, but everyone knew there was tension in the air. We all pretended there was none. Later in the afternoon, Eleanor pulled me aside.

"I though you should know that Paula came back to the hospital in the middle of the night," she confided. "She spent a couple of hours holding Squeaky, giving her a few drops of water at a time with an eye dropper. She didn't get much sleep last night."

Finally, in late afternoon, Squeaky had a bowel movement, and I gave the technicians permission to step up the feeding.

After limping through all of the other office calls that day, I headed to the car, intent to drive home. Once again I remembered the letter to the USDA in the glove compartment. There was no sense in putting this off. I needed to mail the letter no matter how good I felt about Squeaky's progress. So I drove to the bank to visit the same mailbox where I'd mistakenly dropped the bank deposit two months earlier. I sat in the car for a few minutes, reminding myself how stupid and unacceptable that episode had been. Finally, I stepped out of the car and headed for the box, envelope in hand.

As I reached for the handle, a woman approached the bank deposit slot, and we noticed each other.

"Hi, Doc," the suddenly familiar client said. "It's great to see you here! I work for the auto repair shop down the road. I hate it when I have to make these deposits. I'm always worried that I'll lose the envelope or, worse, get mugged with all that cash. I was happy to see your familiar face when I heard someone come up from behind."

I chuckled and soon was telling her about my episode of placing the mail in the bank deposit slot and the bank deposit in the mailbox without even knowing it. I recalled the story of how Steve had summoned me into the post office the next day and had shown me the engagement ring locked in a filing cabinet.

"Don't worry, Doc. You're doing just fine. That new ear medication you gave us for Abby's ears is working great," she said with obvious pride.

"Make sure you keep using it for at least another week," I admonished. "As I recall, Abby's had chronic ear infections for a long time. The most important thing with a new antibiotic is to be sure to use it long enough. Call the office in a week with an update, OK?"

"Thanks, Doc. I'll do that," she promised. "Gotta run! Abby's waiting for me at home, and she always knows if I'm late."

As she headed for her car, I was painfully aware that I had just told her to call the office in a week, not to call me in a week. I wasn't certain I would be there. I reached for the handle on the mailbox one more time. As I did, I noticed a trash can adjacent to the entrance of the bank. Suddenly, I watched as my hands ripped the envelope in half and threw it away. I told myself that I would still mail a letter of inquiry, but that it would be more professional to type a request rather than send a handwritten note.

Squeaky went home three days later, a totally different kitten. She had already gained more than four ounces. She was still gaunt, but she was starting to fill out. I could feel the now excess skin of her abdomen tightening and thickening. When Miss Kimble and her daughter walked into the office to pick up the kitten, the little girl almost jumped into Paula's arms to reclaim her kitten.

"Thanks, Doc!" the little girl shouted in a full, strong voice, so different from that scared squeaky one from just a few days earlier. Her smile traveled from ear to ear.

"Don't thank me," I said as I winked at my technician.

"Thank Paula," I continued. "She's the one who remembered that cats have nine lives."

The little girl held her squirming kitten in one arm and gave Paula's leg a strong hug with the other. Then she took her mother's hand and marched proudly out the door.

Ten days later Squeaky was back in the office for suture removal. Her incision was perfectly healed, and she seemed twice as big. Finally, I allowed myself to believe she might lead a normal life. Plus, the smallest gem of hope began to sprout that I might not be ready to abandon veterinary medicine just yet.

Chapter 14
The Blizzard of '77
West Seneca, January 1977

"Wow! The wind is howling outside," Paula exclaimed. "I've never heard the windows in surgery rattle like that. According to Eleanor, it's almost a total whiteout outside at times."

"Yeah, I can hear the howling, but I'm trying not to focus on it," I said without looking up. "It's taking all the concentration I have to work through this surgery. This is such a delicate procedure. I've amputated the penis and split open what I think is an appropriate length of urethra. Now I am trimming the skin back. Hopefully I'll be able to start putting this jigsaw puzzle back together soon."

"Ever since I came over from human medicine, it's amazed me how many male cats develop urinary crystals," Paula noted. "They end up needing extensive treatment or surgery. Any reason we don't see this as much in other animals, Doc?"

"Well, it can happen in any species, but cats have such a tiny penis that it's more likely for the crystals to cause a blockage. Plenty of female cats develop the same condition, but they have better plumbing, so the crystals pass out with the urine. Sometimes, we see blockages in dogs, but only when the crystals grow much bigger and become stones.

"When you think about it, there is an interesting similarity but also a contrast here to human medicine," I continued. "As you know from your nursing days, people suffer from kidney stones. The acute pain people feel is generally when the small stones travel down and get lodged in the ureter

83

between the kidney and the bladder."

"Yep, I've helped treat people with kidney stones," Paula responded. "They're in excruciating pain. I never thought about how people have most of their problems when the crystals and stones pass from the kidney to the bladder while cats and dogs have problems when the stones travel between the bladder and the outside world."

"I'm sure that no matter where the stones get lodged, the pain is as bad for these poor animals as it is for us," I added as I winced.

"Yep, you're probably right about that," Paula nodded.

It was late January, and by now I had become efficient at doing surgical procedures while carrying on conversations with the technicians as they monitored the depth of anesthesia. The conversations helped take some of the stress out of the situation. This particular surgery, however, was by far the most delicate surgery I had ever attempted. To make matters more intense, this cat belonged to our neighbors who lived right across the street from our home.

"There, that's the last piece of skin I needed to trim," I said. "It's time to start suturing everything back together. This part is critical. If I do a poor job of suturing, the new opening will scar down, and Sam won't be able to pass any other crystals that might form in the future. The surgery will only work if I can make Sam's plumbing look and work more like a Samantha than a Sam. Did you know this surgery basically copies the human sex change procedure?"

Before Paula could respond, there was a loud crackling sound coming from the parking lot. Shelia stuck her head through the surgery door.

"It's that utility pole the car hit the other day," she reported. "The temporary brace Niagara Mohawk put on the pole isn't going to hold up in this wind."

As she spoke, we heard a loud thud as the pole gave way and slammed onto the ground. The power went out. Through the frost-covered window in the suddenly dark surgery room, we heard and saw sparks flying every which way as live electric wires whipped up and down in the parking lot.

"Great! What the heck are we going to do now?" I said, pressing a gauze pad against the incision to prevent bleeding.

"There's a flashlight in the utility closet," Paula remembered. "I'll be right back."

In no time at all she returned and pointed a small light at the incision. I could see the shadowy outline of the incision, but there was not nearly enough light to allow accurate suture placement.

"I've got a big flashlight in the trunk of my car, and it's parked on the other side of the building. I can dash out and get it without getting near those live wires," called Sheila over her shoulder as she headed out into the blizzard. Paula and I stood waiting with the serenading of electrical sparks snapping away in the background.

Sheila, her hair frosted in white snow, was back in less than two minutes. She and Paula pointed both flashlights at the incision from different angles, and I managed to place one suture after another into the incision. My eyes were burning and sore, but thirty minutes later, with Paula's flashlight virtually dead and Sheila's larger flashlight slowly browning out, I placed the last suture. As I tightened the final knot, Paula dashed out the door. I was straining to trim the excess suture from the final knot when Paula reappeared with a penlight from one of the exam rooms to illuminate the incision one final time.

The crackling in the parking lot had stopped. Through the window we could see flashing yellow lights. We knew a Niagara Mohawk crew had arrived and was struggling to tend to the problem. Now that the surgery was over, the lights flickered several times as if to mock us, and then came back on. Apparently, the workers had found a way to kill the power to the flailing wires and at the same time restore electricity to our building.

Soaked with nervous perspiration, I rolled Sam's body gently from side to side to inspect the surgical site. It was far from perfect, but everything appeared to be holding, and small drops of urine were flowing from the surgical site as expected.

"Well, I don't know," I said with a sigh. "This might work, but it might not. I think we did the best we could under the conditions."

"Eleanor just heard on the radio that everything is shut down," Sheila added. "They are already talking about a driving ban for the entire area. The weather department is saying the winds have shifted and the storm is going to be far worse than expected. Buffalo schools have already sent students home and cancelled everything for tomorrow. I can't ever remember them closing the schools a day ahead of time."

"As soon as Sam is awake, you two better hit the road, or you'll never get home," I suggested. "We are probably going to be shut down for a day or two at least. I am going to round up some supplies, take Sam home, and try to treat him there."

Paula and Sheila had every reason to fear a winter storm. Paula had a rare medical condition that caused her fingers to turn blue in cold weather. She wore lightweight gloves even indoors in our poorly heated ancient building. She had been debating between moving to the Southwest to escape the cold of the Buffalo area or possibly having major nerves in her neck surgically severed to help control the problem. Sheila, on the other hand, lived the farthest from the clinic. She generally drove home on the relatively new Route 400 Expressway. However, that highway was almost always the first road officials closed in a snowstorm. That didn't seem to faze Sheila. She simply planned to drive home via Route 16—the old way home.

Both women refused to leave until they knew everything was set for our patient. While I telephoned our neighbors to give an update on Sam's surgery, Paula watched over his recovery from anesthetic. Sheila located a cardboard box and started to collect the supplies needed to treat him at home. The time spent gathering supplies probably cost her dearly as several hours later she ended up stranded at the Springbrook Fire Hall with many other people. Her dedication as a technician and friend caused her to spend the next two days in the fire hall, separated from her newlywed husband.

Sam's owners, our neighbors, were a typical South Buffalo Polish family—two first-generation Americans, Joe and Tina—raising four teenaged boys in a rented old house. Joe had recently lost his job when the steel plants closed down. Nonetheless, this entire family was always upbeat about everything. When I called and explained about treating Sam at home, Tina told me they had a small room right off their kitchen and suggested we set up a makeshift hospital ward there. I agreed that being in familiar surroundings might be better for Sam. It would be no problem for me to cross the street to their house two or three times a day to oversee Sam's care.

Just as Sheila and Paula left the building, Barb pulled in the parking lot in our new red mini-station wagon with both boys returning from ice skating lessons at the YMCA. The snow was already so deep that it almost reached the top of the car's small wheels. We loaded Sam and a box of medical supplies into the back of the car and headed the short half mile home. Across the street, we set up quarters for Sam a few minutes later. I warned Joe and Tina that cats are generally hospitalized for a minimum of two days after this surgery. I also explained that kidney function might not return to normal as his repeated blockages could have taken their toll. I promised to drop by at least twice each day for the next several days to administer fluids and antibiotics. With that, we headed across the street, thankful that we would be able to ride out the storm in our own home. The radio and television reminded us constantly that many people were less fortunate and stranded in many different locations.

Later that night, I trudged back across the unplowed road to examine our patient, and I was concerned when I found Sam still drunken from the anesthetic. Joe and Tina served me a cup of hot cocoa, and I tried hard to mask my disappointment and concern. Joe and Tina were clearly worried too, but they accepted my best efforts without question.

When the alarm went off the next morning, the radio announced the bad news. No one was going anywhere. The winds still howled outside. The usual long list of school closings was replaced by one simple announcement. "All schools are closed." Nonemergency driving was banned throughout the region. The news media had already decided to call the storm The Blizzard of '77, and the national television news reports were showing clips of houses virtually buried under snowdrifts. Some of the video scenes showed highways dotted with mounds of snow created by stranded cars that were no longer visible.

Over a cup of coffee, I could peek across the street when the wind took momentary pause. There were only a few tire ruts through the snow on the road. Tina and Joe's boys were out shoveling their driveway. At 9:00, I dialed

Dr. Tom's home to see how he wanted to handle calls from our answering service, and I learned that he was stranded at the animal hospital. He had not attempted to drive home. He had been involved in a multiple car pileup in a whiteout once before, giving him a healthy fear of snowstorms. I telephoned the office and asked Tom if he needed my help, but he told me to stay home. He would pass the time doing some backlogged paperwork while awaiting a break in the weather. On the rare occasions when the phone rang, he would do his best to help clients by telephone. Since we lived close to the clinic, I offered to take over and do the same once he made it home.

As the boys across the street finished shoveling, I bundled up and headed down the driveway to check on Sam. The cat was only slightly more coherent this morning. Urine seemed to be flowing without problem, an encouraging sign. I couldn't draw blood to see if kidney functions were improving, so progress needed to be assessed on the basis of intuition alone. My lack of experience made that task more difficult. Tina insisted I stay for breakfast, and I was distracted by the boys' excitement over the storm and the prospect of a snow day. They reminded me of my own childhood and romping around in waist-deep snow.

After lunch, I set out to drive to the hospital. Barb wrapped a couple of sandwiches, some fruit, and a quart of milk for Dr. Tom. Our car, with its newly designed front-wheel drive, performed remarkably in the snow. Its low belly and narrow wheelbase didn't fit the existing ruts, but it churned along without complaint. The main road to the hospital was partially plowed, and a few vehicles crept slowly along. Dr. Tom was still at the clinic, with his car completely vanished under a mound of snow. He wouldn't accept a ride home or even help in digging out his car, but he did accept and appreciate the food. As we chatted, the radio declared that all roads were impassable in the direction of his home. Soon the winds began to howl fiercely once more, rattling the windows in the old building. Dr. Tom ordered me to return home for fear the weather might worsen. Like a captain prepared to go down with his ship, he was determined to continue his vigil.

The next morning the weather was only marginally better. Only a few more inches of snow were on the ground, but drifts reappeared faster than the plows could push them aside. To my surprise, our driveway had been faithfully cleared throughout the storm. Initially, I assumed that our landlord had been plowing our driveway. However, as I walked across the street to treat Sam, I noticed that it had been shoveled rather than plowed, and finally I realized that the boys from across the street were shoveling our driveway as well as their own.

I examined the patient nervously. He was finally fully awake and taking some liquids. The surgery site looked better than I had expected. But until Sam's appetite resurfaced, there could be no guarantee his kidneys were doing their thing. Healing did seem to be moving slowly in the proper direction, so I allowed myself some optimism about his chances. I thanked the boys for shoveling our driveway and sheepishly apologized for not recognizing their efforts earlier.

About ten o'clock, Dr. Tom called to say he had finally made it home. The fellow who plowed the animal hospital parking lot had arrived that morning to begin a search for buried parking spaces, and Dr. Tom had accepted a ride home in his four-wheel drive truck. He had informed the answering service to contact me to handle any questions or problems. I promised to give him updates on the snow conditions around the hospital to help decide when we might officially reopen. Conditions were improving slowly, but schools were already canceled for the balance of a week.

Over the next few days, I spoke to numerous clients, giving them advice to deal with problems at home. Occasionally prescriptions could be phoned to their nearest pharmacy. Three patients lived close enough to meet at the clinic for treatments. A fourth patient, a badly lacerated German Shepherd, arrived by snowmobile courtesy of the Buffalo police. Sam gradually recovered, and his appetite returned to normal. By the end of the sixth day, he was well enough that I could discontinue treatments. Sam was yet another example of a cat who had nine lives.

We reopened the clinic one week to the day after Mother Nature had closed it down. Most of the suburbs were clear and functioning, but the National Guard had been called out to help the inner city. Things were worse than in the suburbs for several reasons. Not only was the city equipment older, but also the highway department had been caught with its guard down. A large percentage of its equipment was in for repairs when the storm hit. And, finally, there was simply no place to move the snow. In all, we had just experienced the storm of the century, and Buffalo's reputation for snowy weather was etched in stone forever.

That would seem to end the story of The Blizzard of '77. But personally the story stretched on for another two months. We set a snowfall record that year, as a few more inches appeared on a regular basis, often daily. By late February, the snowbanks at the end of our drive were more than eight feet tall, and for everyone, it was a major chore to throw new snow to the top of the piles. Each morning, Joe and Tina sent their boys over at 6:00 AM to shovel out our drive, despite my pleas for them to stop. There was simply no way that Doc, their trusted neighbor, would have any trouble getting to the office to save other pets. I was only 25, and the handle of "Doc" still felt strange, and the special treatment was embarrassing. But Sam and his family's story represented Barb's and my personal reason for hailing Buffalo's nickname as The City of Good Neighbors.

Chapter 15
The Wizard of Oz
West Seneca, Spring 1977

"Hey, Doc, have you looked at the names on the surgery log today?" asked Paula. "Any idea who you are about to spay?"

"No. Why?" I asked as I positioned surgical drapes over the anesthetized cat on the surgery table.

"You better take a peek at this one and see if you can figure out who it is."

Paula's devilish smile alerted me that there was something unusual about my patient. Then I noticed a small line down the middle of the cat's abdomen. It was a faint surgical scar.

"Squeaky?—No! She can't be this big by now!" I stammered.

"It's Squeaky all right, Doc," Paula beamed. "And she's doing great!"

The surgery took thirty minutes. I reopened the cat's abdomen, removed her left ovary, as well as the left horn of her uterus and the remnant of its right horn. I was not surprised that Squeaky had no right ovary. Just as I had suspected, I had removed it four months earlier.

As I closed the abdomen and accepted that Squeaky was going to make it, I also accepted that I was going to make it as a mature veterinarian. The process had taken nine months. It was as though I'd been through a pregnancy of my own, except that the pain had peaked at midterm rather than at the end. As I placed the final sutures in Squeaky's skin, I sensed I was closing more than her belly. I was closing a most unusual chapter of my life.

By late March, the massive piles of snow that accumulated during the famous blizzard and record-setting snowfall of 1977 were melting away.

And as they did, the last of my concerns and fears were melting with them. I learned new little things almost daily that enhanced and defined my style of practice. Each and every lesson, however, did not occur within the clinic walls.

In early April, Barb needed surgery. She had battled throat infections on and off for almost two years and, finally, her doctor convinced her it was time to remove her tonsils. Tonsillectomy was a relatively routine procedure in children, but for a patient in her twenties, it's a different story. On surgery day, Barb's mother came over to help with the boys, and we headed for the hospital. I had arranged to have the morning off. Barb's surgeon was a retired army doctor with an unusual approach. In adults, he removed tonsils without general anesthesia, using only a local anesthetic spray.

"Such minor surgery," he said. "You'll be fine. The only side effect will be a little sore throat."

Although he sounded so sure of himself, I should have remembered that there is no such thing as minor surgery. Poor Barbara returned to her room just before noon, and in a pathetically raspy voice described her ordeal.

"It was awful," she gurgled. "They placed a blindfold over my eyes, but I could see around it. I could see part of some instrument going into my throat. I gripped the chair handles so hard that it felt like I was in an electric chair about to be executed," she strained to say. "My heart started pounding out of control, and I almost passed out. They stopped and made me put my head in my lap. He yelled at me and said I was going to have a heart attack if I didn't calm down."

"Finally, my pulse slowed and they started again. Then I gagged and coughed so hard that it splattered blood all over the surgeon's glasses. He had to stop a couple of times to wipe them clean."

I winced knowing Barb was never a wimp and rarely complained. Doing the surgery without general anesthetic suddenly didn't seem like such a great idea. I hugged her as best I could, wished her well, and headed for the office.

After office hours that evening, I returned to the hospital to be with her for a few minutes before the end of visiting hours. It was not a pretty sight. Barb started coughing and vomiting up blood just as I walked into her room.

In a flash, her hospital nightgown and bedding resembled a crime scene. Fortunately, a kind-hearted night duty nurse assured us that all of this was normal.

"She'll be fine. You'll see. She just needs a good night's sleep," she said reassuringly. "Things will settle down, and Barb will probably be ready to go home tomorrow."

When I woke up the next morning, I wanted to plan my schedule to be able to pick her up and reunite her with the boys as soon as possible. When I dialed the hospital, I was shocked by the tone of voice coming from the switchboard operator.

"**MERCY HOSPITAL!**" screeched a voice that could only be described as belonging to the Wicked Witch of the West.

"Hi," I replied, trying to be as pleasant as possible. "My wife had surgery yesterday, and I'd like to see how she's doing. Can you connect me to the nursing station on …?"

"**NO—YOU HAVE TO WAIT FOR THEM TO CONTACT YOU!**" interjected the witch, stopping me in midsentence. The phone clicked dead. I shook my head, amazed that her voice had not melted the telephone line. Our practice could never treat our pet-owning clients in such a rude manner. After twenty minutes, I decided to call again, this time with another approach. If nothing else, perhaps a different operator would answer.

"**MERCY HOSPITAL!**" screeched the same demonic voice.

I tried to speak quickly without emotion.

"Dr. Freyburger here. My wife is a patient on Two South. Connect me with the nursing station, please," I directed.

Incredibly, a totally new operator seemed to materialize.

"Certainly, Doctor," she cooed. "Are you in the building?" asked the suddenly Good Witch of the South. (South Buffalo, that is.)

I hesitated. Physicians no doubt didn't use the main switchboard, and my cover might be blown.

"No, but I expect to be there later today," I said, trying to sound confident.

"OK. Here you go. Two South, Doc. Have a great day!" said the very pleasant voice.

Seconds later I was connected with the surgical floor desk, and I introduced myself in the manner that had just worked with the switchboard operator.

"Dr. Freyburger here. My wife is in room 2104. How is she doing?"

The nurse excused herself for a moment and laid the phone on the counter. I could hear shuffling and scurrying in the background. Rather quickly, an older sounding yet clearly nervous voice, perhaps the head nurse, gave me a thorough progress report. Apparently, there was a great deal of shock that a "doctor's" wife was on their floor, and nobody had given them warning.

Thankfully, the update was all good news. Barb was more comfortable than she had been yesterday, and the nurses were waiting for the surgeon to sign the discharge order.

"Would you like me to page him, Doctor?" she asked politely.

"No, that's not necessary. Thanks." I responded quickly.

This time it was my turn to hang up abruptly. I was keenly aware that I was playing the role of the Wizard of Oz, standing behind some curtain marked Doctors Only! I wanted to get off the line before some nurse named Dorothy tugged on the curtain and figured out that I was not a medical doctor.

As I drove to the clinic that morning, I joked to myself that perhaps a dog named Toto would be waiting in need of medical care. Then it occurred to me how powerful the title Doctor tends to be in our society. In most cases that power is appropriate, but in some cases, it is not. By experiencing both phone calls, I understood a little of how some doctors could become intoxicated by the influence of that title. And, sadly, I already knew a few, both medical and veterinary, who were addicted to that power. I vowed to use my title with discretion, to drink it in with moderation, and to guard against any drunken stupor. I also wanted to be certain that our pet owners would always be treated in a manner as far from the first phone call and as close to the second as possible. Some lessons in life come from the most unexpected places.

CHAPTER 16

The Decision

IN MID-APRIL DR. TOM TOOK OFF FOR two weeks with his wife and headed to Hawaii. What a difference in the office compared to the last time he had been away. The practice was running smoothly by then, and I was enjoying the freedom of being in charge. Somehow I had morphed from a green new graduate who believed he'd chosen the wrong career into a reasonably competent veterinarian who looked forward to each day's work. Every night as I dropped the outgoing mail and the bank deposit into their proper slots, I was reminded how far everything had come and how quickly it had happened.

The only negative was that I had a major decision to make. I needed to decide whether to stay on in Dr. Tom's practice or to look for another position. As I analyzed my options, I found many things in favor of staying with the practice. The opportunity that had seemed mediocre a year earlier had paid great dividends, since I had enjoyed the freedom to tackle anything I felt ready to attempt. My surgical skills had progressed far ahead of the game compared to many first-year veterinarians. Twice now, I had experienced handling the practice on my own, which would never have happened in a larger office. Also, I enjoyed excellent working relationships with the staff, especially with Sheila and Paula.

On the negative side, I had a clear sense that a long-term relationship with Dr. Tom was probably not in my future. There were little things that seemed insurmountable. I appreciated many of his business practices, but others I could not accept. While I understood the importance of being frugal, I also recognized there was a fine line between being frugal and being cheap. Dr. Tom would get upset with the staff if they used more than one paper towel to clean an exam table between patients. He never purchased cotton-tipped applicators to clean a pet's ears. We had to twirl a tiny swirl of cotton around a small hemostat and use that since it saved money.

But the real kicker came when the answering service changed their billing practices. Business telephones were suddenly being charged by the call rather than with a flat monthly fee. The answering service had little choice but to impose a ten-cent charge for each call they made to locate the doctor on emergency duty. But Dr. Tom refused to be billed on a call-by-call basis. Instead, he arranged for the answering service to call our homes, let the phone ring only once, and then hang up. We were expected to recognize the single ring and then call in to the answering service for the appropriate message. It was a clumsy and cheap way out of paying a fair fee for a fair service.

"Hi, this is Dr. Freyburger. We were out in the yard, and thought our phone might have rung. Were you trying to reach me?" I asked apologetically.

"No, Dr. Freyburger," responded the answering service operator. I could feel the sense of frustration in her voice as other telephone lines rang in the background. The system was nothing short of embarrassing.

In the end, however, I decided that the positives outweighed the negatives, and I hoped to remain on staff for another year. Most first-year grads were receiving a $2,000 raise to stay on for a second year. I was trying to think like a businessperson, so I decided to ask for a $1,000 raise in salary and an additional $1,000 in benefits rather than salary. There were professional dues, licensing fees, veterinary journal subscriptions, as well as veterinary-society-sponsored disability and term life insurance premiums that could be covered on a pretax basis.

When Dr. Tom returned from his vacation, we met over lunch to discuss the future, and I presented my requests to him.

"I have to admit I'm beginning to enjoy the freedom and extra time with my family," Dr. Tom responded. "All right, it's a deal."

We shook hands and headed back to the office with every expectation that we would be working together for another year.

Several days later, Dr. Tom stood at the scrub sink washing his hands prior to surgery.

"By the way, Pete," he announced casually. "I talked to our accountant the other day, and we won't be able to do those extra things you asked for. Just the raise in base salary. Will you still be staying on?"

I was stunned. Sheila and Paula were nearby prepping a patient for surgery, well within earshot. They were staring at each other in disbelief.

"I'll let you know," I said, walking away. But it was a lie. I knew instantly it was time to move on. I couldn't believe that Dr. Tom had made such a statement in front of other employees. It was a conversation that should have occurred in private, but it was obvious he made the statement in front of others purposefully. And if Tom was unwilling to cover added benefits, then he should at least have offered me more of a raise in base salary. I knew that I would be a strong asset to Dr. Tom's practice if I stayed, but since he failed to understand the value of retaining me on his staff, it was time to look elsewhere. I felt embarrassed for Sheila and Paula. I was certain they realized that everything would spiral downhill after that all-too-public announcement.

That night, I scoured through the classified ads in the most recent veterinary journal. Nothing interesting jumped out. Two days later, on my day off, I drove to Ithaca to visit the student placement office at the veterinary college. Any new listings would show up there long before they would make it into the journals. My efforts were rewarded. In Niagara County, a well-known practice twenty miles north of Buffalo had a new listing and was advertising for two veterinarians. The ad noted that the owner hoped to retire soon, so partnership or buyout potential was available. That seemed odd. I had heard that the original owner had a reputation for being a bit eccentric, but I also knew that two younger veterinarians had become partners in the practice. Apparently, things had not worked out. Nonetheless, it looked like an excellent opportunity for me to work in a different type of practice with exposure to new ideas and new approaches to veterinary medicine. Any potential to become a partner or to purchase the practice was clearly a plus. I scribbled down the telephone number and headed back to Buffalo.

The next day during lunch, I went home to call the Lockport practice. Ironically, I had misplaced the slip of paper with the phone number, so I grabbed the telephone directory and turned to the veterinarian listings in the Yellow Pages. The practice had no listing in the Buffalo area phonebook, which seemed very odd. I knew the practice was located a few miles into Niagara County, placing it in a different telephone district, but it had to attract pet owners from the Buffalo area. I called directory assistance to locate the number, and I was given a Niagara County number, which I knew was a long distance call for anyone in Erie County. Most of the businesses in that area provided a second Erie County phone number for the convenience of customers on the Buffalo side of the county line. As I dialed the number provided, I made a mental note to address that problem if hired. The owner was not in, but the receptionist took my name and home phone number and promised he would call me back that evening.

It took three days, but finally I received a call from the owner of the clinic in Niagara County.

"Hi," said the doctor on the other end of the telephone. "Everyone uses my nickname Red, so please do the same."

He continued on with great pride telling me he had already hired a former veterinary school classmate, Dr. Jason, who would be joining the practice in six weeks when his postgraduate surgical internship at a veterinary college ended. I didn't know Jason well but remembered that he had associated with students who were interested in equine medicine. Since large animals were no longer treated by this practice, his interest in Red's practice seemed unusual, but I had no reservations about working with him. Since Red was hoping to hire an additional veterinarian, we scheduled a meeting the following Thursday afternoon.

The hospital was a large one-story brick building set well back from the highway and tucked behind Red's massive colonial-style white house. A large parking lot spread out behind the house but in front of the animal hospital. I found Dr. Red inside a white picket fence, tending to a large garden to the left of the hospital building. He was a tall, white-haired, grandfatherly figure with the stub of a burned-out cigar crushed into the corner of his mouth. He was wearing a blue coverall jumpsuit with his name embroidered above the chest pocket, looking far more like a farm veterinarian than a small animal veterinarian.

"Come on in," he invited. "I'm trying to get some of the garden in early this year. Each spring I work in all the ashes from the crematory," he said, pointing to the smokestack on the side of the building. "The extra minerals are great for the flowers and the vegetables."

We had used a pet burial service at Dr. Tom's office, so this was a bit new to me. I didn't doubt that the ashes would help the garden, but I wondered just how many ashes one plot of ground could take. I also wondered if most pet owners were aware of this final resting place for their beloved pets.

"Ashes to ashes and dust to dust," I said with a forced smile, using the only response I could ad-lib.

As we toured the hospital, the waiting room caught my attention. A prominent wooden airplane propeller hung on the wall. Apparently, Red had acquired his nickname while in the military during World War II. At first I wasn't certain if the name came from the color of his hair in his youth or from a comparison to the famous Red Baron from World War I. Red chewed the cigar a bit harder as he talked of his time in the military. I soon learned the nickname he lived by was due to his wartime skills as a pilot. His road to veterinary medicine had been on the GI bill after the war. While I could already sense a bit of his eccentric personality, I found myself liking a guy who had served his country proudly and returned home to find success after the war.

We finished touring the hospital and went out back to see his barn. He raised racing ponies and competed in pony harness racing around the state. I didn't even know ponies were used for racing. He also raised homing pigeons that he took on the road when racing and then released for exercise as they flew home.

He was supposed to be interviewing me, but in truth, I rarely got a word in edgewise as he spoke almost nonstop. It seemed like every other sentence was about Jason and how excited he was to have hired a veterinarian who had just finished an internship. It was clear that I would be playing second fiddle if hired, but that didn't bother me. Internships like the one Jason was about to finish were both difficult and rare, so it made sense that Red was excited and that Jason would get top billing.

We ended the interview, and Red promised to call in a few days to let me know if he would offer me a position. I sensed that he likely wanted to ask Dr. Jason if he had any reservations about working with me before making a commitment. From my perspective, this practice seemed like an ideal change in professional scenery as well as a new and challenging opportunity. So I expressed an interest and thanked Red for the interview.

CHAPTER 17

Meeting Dr. Phil Weber
Lockport, May 1977

AS I LEFT THE DR. RED'S OFFICE, I met Dr. Phil Weber, a relief veterinarian, as he left the hospital. He was spending most of his time in the Rochester area but was filling in at Red's practice on available days. Because the idea of relief veterinarians was quite new in the field of veterinary medicine, and because Phil had worked in so many other practices around the northeast, I seized the opportunity to ask him a few questions.

It was difficult to judge his age as we talked. He was bald with whitish sideburns and a white mustache. But he was outgoing and upbeat, with a playful youthfulness to his presence. It didn't take more than a moment for me to realize that he had that rare charismatic personality that instantly bonded him to everyone he met. We talked for about fifteen minutes in the parking lot. As the conversation went on, I learned that he was in his midforties. I learned that Phil had owned a practice near Elmira that he had sold several years earlier. He'd been through a divorce in a small town and had decided it was best to move on. Rather than settling in elsewhere to start a new practice, he made the decision to travel around doing relief work. He was beginning to think about owning a new practice elsewhere but was enjoying the nomadic life style in the interim. Since all this meant that he had worked in many different situations, I figured he would have good insight into the conditions at this practice. I started probing.

"You're right, Red is a tad eccentric," Phil said with a chuckle. "You will find he's got a bit of a dual personality. Away from the clinic he's the kind of fellow who would give you the shirt off his back. Around the clinic he's a different guy. But he's harmless. Pretty much all he wants to do are a few office calls and ear crops. He's proud of his ear crops. And he does a good job. But as you know, cropping is gradually fading in popularity. Beyond that, he doesn't do any other surgery. His real joy in life is playing with those darn ponies. I guess he's been around long enough to have earned the right to do that.

"Overall, this hospital practices good medicine," Phil continued. "I think it's an excellent opportunity for someone your age. You will get to do a lot, and sooner or later, he may see the light and decide to retire altogether. Apparently, the last partnership fell apart because he wasn't ready to step away as soon as the new partners hoped, and his involvement eventually drove a wedge between them. My understanding is that they were both from the Midwest, and they decided to pull the plug on the deal to return home.

"If you land here and eventually talk to him about ownership, my only advice would be to buy him out totally," he warned. "Avoid any partnership arrangement."

"Wow! Thanks," I said. "I really appreciate your willingness to talk about this openly. That's very helpful."

"You're on the right track asking me questions about the practice rather than asking him," Phil said. "Most young grads aren't smart enough to do that. Good luck, Pete!"

Phil and I instantly liked each other but never expected to meet again, as our paths in life were so different. Neither of us had a clue how our futures would intertwine down the road.

CHAPTER 18

New Position

West Seneca and Lockport, May 1977

"HI. THIS IS RED. I'M STILL INTERESTED in offering you a job. But I'd like to meet your wife first. I've hired a lot of vets over the years, and eventually they all move on. I think in most cases the women are the ones who are the problem. I'd like to meet your wife before making a commitment."

"OK. That's not a problem," I responded. "We can arrange to come up any evening except Monday. Is any day better for you?"

"Thursday around eight would be good. Can you make it then?" he asked.

"Sure. See you then," I responded.

Red's telephone call had come four days later than promised, and I had just about given up hope of landing a position at his hospital. In the meantime, I had learned from some colleagues that Red had lost more than twenty associates over the years. Red apparently always wanted to blame the wives rather than deal with the reality that he might be any part of the problem. Nonetheless, I was ready for new scenery, and I was willing to play the game on his terms if necessary.

On the following Thursday evening, as Red walked us around the clinic, I noticed right away that he was pointing out totally different things to Barbara than he had pointed out to me on my previous visit. In the first exam room, he pulled open a small drawer.

"We keep the Bazooka bubble gum in a drawer like this in each of the exam rooms," he beamed. "I absolutely insist on giving bubble gum to children who come in with their parents. I know it works because many of them are now grown and are bringing their pets. They always remember the bubble gum I gave out when they were young."

Red was already heading down the hall as Barb and I exchanged glances. We were both thinking the same thing. There were only three veterinary practices in this small town, so many of the clients would have come back even without the gum. Also, mothers these days were concerned about tooth decay, and they probably didn't like it that a doctor, even if he was a vet, gave their children anything sugary without permission. I could also sense Barb curling her nose at the large built-in ashtrays hanging from the wall in each exam room. I hadn't noticed them, but they were clearly for Red's cigar butts.

When we reached the back of the building, Red took us into a small room off the main surgery.

"This is where I do all the ear crops. See that over there?" he said, pointing to an antique-looking piece of equipment. "That's a hot motor oil sterilizer I use for my ear cropping instruments. The oil keeps the blades razor sharp. Military dentists used these during the war. No one is allowed to touch any of this. Not even the technicians. I take care of it myself. You guys use that new steam sterilizer down the hall in the lab. It's OK, but it dulls the sharp edges on scissors and scalpels."

"That's interesting," I said, trying to hide my astonishment. "I've never heard of oil sterilization." I tried to imagine why anyone would want to handle instruments sterilized in hot motor oil. Again Barb and I exchanged glances as we turned to catch up to Red who was already halfway down the next hallway. We were supposed to be here for Red to meet and get to know Barb, but once again it seemed that only the opposite was true.

"Are you sure you want to work for this guy?" Barb asked on the way home. "He seems a bit different to say the least."

"Absolutely!" I responded. "The practice is far better equipped than Tom's, and Red was once on the cutting edge of veterinary medicine. Over the years his associates have kept everything up-to-date, even if he's fallen behind the times. The pharmacy has all kinds of medications I don't have access to now. There's a real surgery room with a real surgery light rather than a converted old garage. And the lab has modern diagnostic equipment.

"Red is eccentric, but he's harmless at the same time," I continued. "I think he's on his way out and he knows it. He will need to get serious about retiring at some point soon. If things work out here, all the better. If not, it will make a nice stepping stone to opening our own practice."

Ten days went by without a call. Once again, I assumed Red had decided against offering me a job and, once again, I began scouting around for other opportunities. I was truly surprised when, eleven days after our last conversation, Red telephoned and offered me the position. The offer was only for $500 a year more than Dr. Tom had offered and undoubtedly was for less than he had offered Jason. Nonetheless, I accepted the offer and agreed to start on July 1.

Since it would soon be June, and I felt obligated to give Dr. Tom a full month's notice, I needed to talk to Dr. Tom the very next day. Resigning turned out to be one of the hardest things I had ever done. I was truly attached to Paula and Sheila and sincerely appreciated the opportunity Dr. Tom's practice had provided. When I informed Dr. Tom, it took him by surprise, and he too warned me about Red's history with other associates. Yet he realized my mind was set, and he accepted my resignation.

"You haven't taken any of your two weeks vacation, but we are starting into the busy season. Will you be able to work straight through until July 1?" he asked.

"Sure, no problem," I responded. I felt I owed him that much and that the two extra weeks vacation pay I would receive at the end of the month would come in handy with our moving expenses.

To his credit, on my last scheduled day, Dr. Tom closed the office for two hours and took the entire crew out to lunch as a farewell gesture. However, as I left the office that day for the last time, he handed me an envelope with my final paycheck, and it did not contain any vacation pay. I had just learned another valuable lesson in how not to treat employees in the future.

CHAPTER 19

Second Fiddle
Lockport, Summer 1977

"HI, MRS. HOPKINS," SAID RED WITH a huge grin punctuated by the soggy butt of a cigar. "I want you to meet our new associate, Dr. Jason. He just finished special surgical training at a veterinary college. And, oh, there's another new staff vet, Dr. Pete, back there somewhere."

Red stayed in the waiting room for two hours on our first day on the job so that he could tell his clients about his new vets. He kept pulling Jason out of exam rooms to introduce him to clients with special pride. Ironically, he kept Jason so busy socializing with the clients that I ended up seeing most of them and their pets in the exam rooms. That was fine with me. The pressure was all on Jason, and he certainly deserved top billing. I preferred to meet the clients over the exam room table rather than in the waiting room.

The exam tables in Red's hospital were marble topped-desks rather than the higher exam tables used in most veterinary clinics. That meant the veterinarian sat on a chair at the desk as he examined the pet. I immediately liked that approach as it felt less formal and seemed to put the clients more at ease. The doctor and the client were on the same level. This seemed to fit perfectly with my low-key approach to greeting clients and their pets. When owners came in with a pet, I had already adopted a style of greeting the pet first rather than the owner, similar to the way I greeted children first. Although unorthodox, my approach always seemed to earn the respect of the pet owners. So as Red was introducing Jason with his approach, I was introducing myself as I preferred.

Things might have progressed better if I had managed to stay out of Red's way as much as he was staying out of mine. After a couple of hours, Red tired of introducing Jason to each and every client. Once again, he reminded both of us that it was essential to hand bubble gum to each child. He was apparently ready to turn his attention to his prized racing ponies when the first accident happened. As Red headed down the pharmacy hallway, I was reading the label on a bottle of a new type of injectable antibiotic. It seemed an excellent choice for the dog I was examining whose kidney infection had persisted despite treatment with several standard antibiotics. As I turned back toward the exam room, I saw Red in my peripheral vision, and I shifted my stance to avoid a collision. As I moved, the bottle slipped from my hand and hit the floor, smashing between our feet.

"Oh dear, I'm sorry about that," I said, knowing that it was by far the most expensive item in the pharmacy.

"Don't understand why you young fellows need that expensive new stuff," Red muttered in a huff as he continued to walk. "Penicillin works just fine, and it doesn't cost an arm and a leg."

Twenty minutes later, I watched Red in the parking lot. He was chewing his trademark cigar and training one of his ponies on a lunge line. His routine created an obstacle for each and every car in or out of the practice's parking lot, but Red just waved and smiled at all of them, totally oblivious to the annoyed looks etched on the faces of some of the clients. Others found the scene cute, but only until it delayed their plans.

I had started the morning playing second fiddle to Jason. Clearly, after breaking the bottle of expensive medication, I had fallen to some position lower than second fiddle in a few short hours. I was all but ignored for the next two weeks. However, on the morning before a noon staff meeting, Red acted differently toward me. He actually started a conversation with me, and he even introduced me to a couple of the longtime clients as they entered the waiting room. I could not figure out why I had suddenly appeared on his radar screen after being virtually ignored.

At the staff meeting, he called everyone into his large office and perched himself behind his lavish desk like a king, with the remainder of the staff, including Jason and me, seated on folding chairs in the periphery of the room. When he started the meeting, he reached into a desk drawer and pulled out a three-page letter written by one of the clinic's long-term clients. She bred poodles and ran a small grooming business out of her home several miles down the road. He read every word of the letter out loud to the employees.

The entire letter was about me, with the client raving about how I had taken the time to explain how tear production in the eyes worked, why I had chosen a particular eye medication for her dog, and how I expected the medication would work. She noted that several of her dogs had been treated for eye infections over the years, but no one had ever taken the time to explain how things worked and why one medication was better than another. She spent most of the last page congratulating Red for bringing someone like me onto the staff. Now the entire staff knew why I was suddenly the focus of attention.

Listening to the lengthy letter was embarrassing and way over the top for a staff meeting. I would have much preferred that he referenced the letter and perhaps posted it on the bulletin board, where other client thank-you notes were often posted. Nevertheless, after just two weeks on the job and after a rocky start, it appeared I was on a bit more of an equal footing with Jason, thanks to the letter.

CHAPTER 20

The C-Section
Lockport, Fall 1977

"THAT DOESN'T LOOK GOOD! WHAT'S UP?" I said to Cheryl and Ben one Thursday morning as I entered the building. They were carrying a stretcher. An obviously distressed spaniel was lying on its side, struggling to breathe.

"It's Ginger, Mr. Macintyre's prize-winning Brittany," answered Cheryl. "Dr. Jason did an emergency C-section on her in the middle of the night two days ago. She's eight years old, so they decided to do a hysterectomy at the same time. But she hasn't acted right since. The family found her unable to walk this morning."

Cheryl was the head veterinary technician in Red's practice. Her family ran a vegetable farm and raised pigs in the rich farmland below the Niagara escarpment. She had chosen to be a veterinary technician rather than work the fields with the other members of her family. However, her farming background meant she was as tough as nails and no stranger to hard work. Ben was our dependable handyman who did countless odd jobs around the hospital and in the pony barn. He had worked for Red for many years.

I quickly examined the dog and then headed out into the waiting room to confer with the owner.

"Good morning, Mr. Macintyre," I said, introducing myself. "Dr. Jason isn't here today. I understand he did a C-section on Ginger two nights ago. How long has Ginger been down like this?"

"We found her that way this morning," he responded. "She was up and walking last night, but even then she seemed to be in a great deal of pain despite the surgery. She hasn't eaten a thing. Last night she tried to nurse her pups, but she wouldn't let them nurse this morning. She's been a great dog—our best ever. She won a dual state championship—both bench and field trial—four years ago. We knew her breeding days were about over, and we're training several nice pups she's thrown over the years. But we expected she'd be with us for a longer time than this. We can't let her suffer. You better put her down, and we'll hand-raise this litter of pups."

"Well, that may be all we can do," I agreed. "But all the pain seems localized in the abdomen back near her pelvis. I'm going to take her back to surgery and open her up. Perhaps some of the sutures failed to hold, or there's some damage to her bladder. It's a long shot, but I want to be sure before we put her down. You head home and help the family hand-feed her puppies. I imagine you have your hands full at the moment. If I get her opened up and there is nothing we can do, we will euthanize her on the table without waking her up. Go home and hope for the best, but prepare the family for the worst. I'll be in touch soon."

"OK, Doc. You folks have never steered us wrong in the past," he said. "All I can do is leave the decision in your hands."

A half hour later, Cheryl had Ginger secured to the surgery table and anesthetized. Her belly was scrubbed and ready. The incision from two nights ago was almost hidden in a valley between the mountains of her milk-engorged mammary glands. As I was donning surgical gloves, Red poked his head into the room.

"Looks like Jason somehow screwed this one up," he grumbled. "The Macintyres have been great clients since we opened our doors. Chances are we'll lose them over this mess. Ben said the dog is on its way out, so you might as well put her down."

"I'm not certain what went wrong," I said with a shrug. "At first I thought it might be milk fever, but she hasn't been shaking, and her temperature is normal. She shows pain in the posterior abdomen, so I'm going to take a peek. I'm certain Jason would open her up if he was here today."

"Sounds like a waste of time, but suit yourself. Whatever damage was done, it's too late now," Red said as his voice trailed down the hall toward the rear exit.

I was beginning to understand Red's approach to things, and I knew that he wouldn't want to be involved when we ultimately decided to put Ginger down. He headed off to play with his ponies as I started the surgery. First I removed the skin sutures and carefully released sutures in the muscle layer one by one. As I did, a small balloon like structure started to rise out of the incision.

"What the heck is that?" Cheryl asked.

"I'm not certain," I said as I continued to release sutures. As more of the gas-filled membrane came out of the incision, I added, "There's a suture line here and it seems to be holding so far. This has to be the uterine stump, all bloated for some reason. Grab a syringe so we can remove some of the gas to see what's going on."

I drew several large syringes full of gas out of the thin balloonlike structure. We could smell a putrid odor each time I emptied the syringe and gradually deflated the grotesque balloon. I was drawing out gas rather than liquid, but the similarity to the surgery I had done on Squeaky eight months earlier came to mind. After deflating most of the tension, I made a small incision into the stump and inserted a finger.

"Oh, dear God. I was afraid of that!" I exclaimed.

"What is it?" asked Cheryl.

"I'm pretty certain I feel the bloated nose of a dead puppy stuck in the birth canal. The gas and the smell are coming from the rotting tissues." I gently enlarged the incision in the stump, and then I worked a forceps up into the birth canal. I could touch the tip of the nose of the dead puppy, but I couldn't get the forceps to grab anything solid.

"Pull on an exam glove, lube up your finger, and insert it in Ginger's vagina like we do in a pelvic exam," I said to Cheryl. "That will push everything forward in my direction as far as possible. Hopefully I can grab it and try to work it out this way."

Cheryl had no problem following the instructions and never mentioned the foul odor that was now permeating the surgery room.

"Generally, a dog of this age needs a C-section due to uterine inertia,"

I lectured as we worked. "The muscles of the uterus just won't contract properly. But the surgeon is always supposed to check the birth canal in a dog this size to make certain there is not a pup lodged up there. In the middle of the night, doing the surgery by himself without a technician or anyone else to help, Jason must have forgotten to do that. Or he may have checked and not felt anything as this pup is in a breach position in the canal. I could only feel the tip of the nose, and the fetus is probably bloated quite a bit larger than it was at the time of surgery."

As I talked, I managed to hook the forceps firmly onto the dead puppy's lower jaw, and I gently rocked it back and forth trying to free it. It took at least five minutes, but it slowly released, and finally the puppy slithered out of the incision. It was a gross, smelly thing, badly deformed by the gasses released from the decaying tissue.

"There!" I said. "This pup has been dead for several days and clearly was dead before the C-section."

"Wow!" Cheryl exclaimed, "Did you notice how the heartbeat on the monitor smoothed out and slowed down as soon as the pup came free?"

"Yes, I noticed. Pretty cool, isn't it?" I offered. "Even though Ginger is under anesthesia and has no conscious perception of pain, the nervous system still senses the pressure. There was pain even at a subconscious level."

"Will she be all right?" Cheryl asked.

"I'm not certain, but let's hope so." I said. "Obviously we'll need to cover her heavily with antibiotics to prevent peritonitis or even mastitis if she survives and continues to produce milk. And I'll have a limited choice of antibiotics. I have to use one that won't harm the nursing puppies. We also have to watch for any nerve damage to the hind legs. There is an important nerve that lies on both sides of the pelvic canal. If it's damaged, the legs splay out, and the animal can't pull them back toward the center of the body. It's called obturator paralysis. It's an extremely rare problem in dogs but a common cause of downer cows on dairy farms after a difficult calving."

"Oh yeah. I saw that happen to a cow on our neighbor's farm," Cheryl noted. "Red is going to be furious when he finds all this out. How are you going to handle all that?" Cheryl asked.

"I'm not certain," I responded. "Our first priority is to get Ginger back up and home. After that, I'll try to use this case as an example of why we need a better facility for emergency care. A group of hospital owners down in Buffalo are meeting once a month, trying to form a veterinary emergency clinic. Emergency clinics are springing up on the West Coast, and Buffalo could have one of the first facilities on the East Coast if things go well. They hire vets who focus on after-hours care. They typically open at six each evening and close at eight in the morning. They are also open weekends and holidays, so clients can always have access to good quality, round-the-clock emergency care."

"Hmm, that's different," Cheryl muttered. "Do you think our clients will drive all the way to Buffalo for care on nights and weekends?"

"Naturally there will be resistance to change," I agreed. "But once clients understand the benefits, they'll accept change. Let's face it. Emergency care at most veterinary hospitals around the country is too limited. How much can a doctor do in the middle of the night? If a dog comes in hit by a car, pretty much all we can do is give it medication for shock and cover it with antibiotics. Badly bleeding wounds are bandaged. After that, all we can do is put it in a cage and head home for some sleep. If the pet is alive in the morning, we start doing X-rays and so on. If it dies during the night, we would like to think that we did everything we could, and that's what we tell the owner, but it certainly is not the level of care people get when they end up in a hospital. Pet owners have been satisfied with our approach up until now, but you can see the writing on the wall. Owners are placing more and more value on their pets. They won't find it acceptable much longer. And let's face it. It would be almost impossible for all veterinary hospitals to monitor pets around the clock, and an emergency clinic could do that, too. I think that we should all cooperate on this one, and we'll all be helping each other, the pet owners and the pets. Everybody wins in the long run. That's how I see it."

"That makes a lot of sense, but I doubt Red will be interested," responded Cheryl.

"I know," I sighed. "But at least I can use this case as an example of why better emergency care is important. That will help take the focus off any surgical error, for Jason's sake, too."

We talked nonstop until Ginger was sutured back together.

"Great job, Doc! That was really wild. I have to admit—I didn't think there was anything we could do. Look, she's waking up."

"Thanks Cheryl, but I'm certain Jason would have done the same and would have preferred to find and correct his own error," I pointed out. "It could just as easily be the other way around next time something goes wrong."

Chapter 21
Golden Boy
Lockport, Fall 1977

GINGER WENT HOME THAT AFTERNOON even though she could not walk properly. She was still producing milk and needed to be with her puppies if there was to be any chance of her continuing to nurse. I kept in touch with the Macintyres daily by telephone. It was several days until things returned to normal, but helping her get around the house was much less work than hand feeding her four puppies. Fortunately, she never developed post-op infection, had no lasting nerve damage, and made a full recovery.

Despite my efforts to downplay the incident, Red's attitude marked a major change in office dynamics. Suddenly I was his new golden boy who he hoped would join the practice as a partner and become his eventual successor. Jason, despite his superior surgical training, became the afterthought. I was amazed by the 180-degree shift that had happened in just a few short months. I had a sense that both Jason and I were excellent young vets destined to be successful. As such, I would have preferred more equal treatment. But Red was not about to see things that way.

As Cheryl predicted, I could not generate any real interest in Red to support the concept of a regional animal emergency clinic. However, since you had to be a practice owner to participate in the meetings in Buffalo, he did allow me to attend the meeting as his representative. At the same time, I was quickly taking on other management tasks within the hospital normally handled by the practice owner. I took charge of the drug ordering, started interviewing prospective new employees, and began to handle most of the cases involving emotionally stressed clients. Remembering my initial difficulty telephoning this clinic from the Buffalo area, I began researching how we could improve that situation. Eventually I was also able to get Red to install a Buffalo-area telephone number for the convenience of pet owners on the other side of the county line. He believed it was a waste of money, but eventually allowed the project to go forward. It was an instant success, as our business from Erie County showed very noticeable improvement.

One evening, while covering emergencies, I was called to the office to see a litter of dachshund puppies I had vaccinated that afternoon. They all had severe allergic reactions to the vaccine, and their faces were swollen almost beyond recognition. They were all struggling to breathe. I spent three hours that night at the hospital giving them tiny doses of antihistamine and cortisone to counteract the anaphylactic reaction to the vaccine, and while I tended the delicate little pups, I had time to get to know their owners. Finally, the pups' breathing improved, and I sent them home to wait for the remainder of the reaction to wear off. It seemed clear there had to be some genetic connection to the allergic reaction to the vaccine since all six puppies had the same bad reaction. The very next day I read in a veterinary journal how certain breeds were developing bad reactions to the one particular portion of the standard puppy combination vaccines. Dachshunds were the number one breed on the list. Since that particular disease had not been seen in the northeast for decades, and since the risk of the vaccine was now outweighing the risks of the disease, many specialists were recommending a switch to a vaccine without that portion. Having been given the job of drug ordering, I changed the hospital vaccine protocol the very next day.

Not all of my responsibilities suited the dignity of my profession. Whenever I tended to emergencies at night, one of the things I recognized was that the hospital was badly infested with cockroaches. When I opened a drawer in the exam rooms to find scissors or bandaging material, ugly bugs would scurry out everywhere, right in front of the pet owner. And yes, the drawer that was full of bubble gum contained the most roaches, so I quickly learned to avoid that drawer. As soon as I could, I called in and interviewed several exterminators. Even though Red once again felt I was being extravagant, spending money needlessly, we hired one of them. The problem quickly came under control, and we established a relationship with the exterminator service. Soon we were referring pet owners with serious flea problems to the service since no effective flea medications were available in the 1970s. Some of these pet owners were finding real relief from flea infestations for the first time in years.

I had only been in practice for fifteen months, yet already I had become a competent surgeon. I had developed a knack for establishing good rapport with even hard-to-handle clients. I had initial management experiences. Additionally, I had begun rubbing elbows with the established hospital owners in the Buffalo area. My career was moving forward, and my self-confidence was soaring.

While I was happy and comfortable with how things were progressing, Jason was just as unhappy. While the two of us were getting along without any problem whatsoever, it was apparent that he and Red were not in a comfortable working relationship. I knew by then that Jason had taken the job hoping to buy the practice and reintroduce equine work, his number one interest. Since it was clear that would not happen, I fully expected that he would be moving on at the end of his contract year. We were all stunned, however, when he gave thirty days notice that he was moving on after only five months on the job. He had purchased a small practice elsewhere in the state. It was closer to his childhood home, and it was an excellent spot to offer equine services. I was saddened to see him move on so quickly but happy for the opportunity he had found. The fact that he had managed to move his career to the next level despite the awkward six-month stay in Red's practice helped to keep my own desire to own a practice fresh and alive.

Once Jason moved on, I was truly Red's golden boy. Barb and I were uncomfortable in the small house we were renting on a month-to-month basis, so Red offered us a large farmhouse that he owned. Many of his best associates had lived there over the years, and Dr. Jason and his family had just vacated the home. We accepted the offer and moved to nicer surroundings.

I had an interest in buying Red's practice but only if he was ready to step aside altogether. And it was clear that he was not ready to do that, so it was time for Barb and me to begin thinking about our future.

CHAPTER 22
Working with Dr. Phil
Lockport, Winter 1978

ABOUT A MONTH AFTER JASON DEPARTED, Red once again hired Dr. Phil Weber, who had been at the practice doing relief work on the day of my initial interview. Dr. Phil was getting bored with the vagabond life of a relief veterinarian and wanted to settle down in a practice of his own once again. While he was researching various possibilities, he had agreed to work for Red for the next few months while Red searched for another young veterinarian to replace Jason.

Phil and I immediately enjoyed working together. We shared similar philosophies and goals in life. We each saw a bit of ourselves in the other. And we discussed everything openly and without reservation. I had confidence that I was a good surgeon. However, I soon learned that Phil was a great surgeon. He had even stayed on at Cornell for an extra year after graduation, working as a surgical instructor.

"Who taught you how to do spays?" he asked cautiously one day after watching my techniques.

"Well, let's see," I responded. "I did a few spays as a senior. Then after that I was pretty much on my own in surgery. So I guess the style I use is pretty much self-taught. Why?"

"Would you be insulted if I gave you a couple of simple tricks that would make your life easier?" he asked cautiously.

"Absolutely not! Fire away." I welcomed any advice from someone who obviously had far more talent in surgery.

Phil proceeded to show me some techniques I had never seen. They were very simple changes in my style that noticeably decreased the time it took me to do various surgeries. Over the next few weeks, I learned more about the fine points of surgery than I had under Dr. Tom or Red's tutelage in a year and a half. Also, since Phil had worked in many different practices as a relief veterinarian, he had picked up many tips on procedures, equipment, and different ways of doing things. I encouraged him to share the best of those ideas, and slowly we introduced many to Red's practice.

During his months of relief work in the Rochester area, Phil had also become a hockey fan. I had played hockey in my youth and had always been a big fan of the sport. The two of us began attending Buffalo Sabres games on a regular basis, sitting way up in the orange seats in Memorial Auditorium. During the games, I explained the finer details of the sport to Phil. During the intermissions, Phil shared his research on other practices he was considering purchasing. He was not inclined to stay in the Buffalo area. He felt the region was too economically depressed to be a good location for a practice. He was investigating one practice for sale near Philadelphia and another in the Corning area. He was also researching the possibility of starting a new practice in the vicinity of Rochester since that area had better economical footing thanks to the presence of large, modern corporations such as Kodak and Xerox. Phil was also working with a veterinary practice management consultant in the Ithaca area. The consultant was using demographic data to pinpoint a good location for a new practice or the future potential for an existing practice. I was fascinated with this relatively new approach, and I started to apply the same principles to the Buffalo area.

One day, I spent a few hours at the Niagara Frontier Planning Commission headquarters, collecting demographic data to check out the potential locations in Erie and Niagara County. When I showed the data to Phil, he was certain I had made an error in the calculations. The Buffalo area appeared to be a more favorable area than the Rochester area based on an average of the number of veterinarians in the area on a per capita basis, even when adjusted for average household income. Phil decided to do some research to double- check my findings. The demographic data from the planning board had population figures for most of the large cities in New York State, so Phil spent an afternoon in downtown Buffalo, at the main county library, going through telephone books for the Rochester, Syracuse, and Albany areas, counting the number of veterinarians. The figures were undeniable. The potential for success was clearly greater in the Buffalo area than in any of the other upstate cities despite the economic challenges of the region.

For the first time, Phil began to think about settling down somewhere in the Buffalo area. He and I began to talk about the possibility of either buying Red's practice together or finding a good location to start a new practice together. Fate had brought the two of us together, and fate had pointed Phil in a different direction than he might ever have imagined.

CHAPTER 23

Scott David
Lockport, Spring 1978

AFTER WE MOVED TO LOCKPORT, life slowed to a crawl for Barbara. She was accustomed to a very busy lifestyle, either as a student, a worker, or most recently, a young mother. Suddenly Brian was in first grade and gone most of the day. Todd's speech development was delayed, so he was attending a special preschool program twenty miles away. With a long bus ride in both directions, he too was absent much of the time. For a large part of each day, Barb's only companion was Mitzie, a German Shorthair Pointer we had adopted after the Blizzard of '77. She was a great dog, but her one flaw was that she could not be confined. We had an excellent dog kennel attached to the side of the garage, but it was useless. Mitzie was one of the small number of dogs that had learned to climb chain-link fencing, using her elbows and rear feet to scale the six-foot fence seemingly without effort. She was also fascinated with bugs and insects of all types. If she managed to get outdoors, she always headed to her favorite place, an old abandoned apple orchard behind the farmhouse, where a local beekeeper housed beehives. We could always find Mitzie standing in front of one of the hives snapping at bees flying into or out, shaking her head violently after being stung, and then returning for more. Barb spent a great deal of time retrieving Mitzie from the orchard.

Barb had never lived in as rural a location as this home, and she found it uncomfortable. First, there were no close neighbors. There were none on the other side of the road. There were no neighbors to the north. There were several neighbors to the south, but the closest home was separated from our house by an eighty-acre cornfield. Second, the fields around the farmhouse caused Barb's pollen allergies to soar. And not only the fields but also our old farmhouse made her sneeze. The foundation of the house was made with hand-laid stone, and the basement contained an antiquated rainwater cistern, a remnant from the days before public water was available. The entire basement was dark, damp, and musty, producing untold numbers of mold spores that played havoc on her allergies. In short, Barb was experiencing an uncomfortable period in her life.

To complicate things, she was pregnant once again. But pregnancy meant that she could not take her allergy medication, and for a while it looked like she would have a miserable nine months. Yet, somehow, Mother Nature always seems to provide a way to protect pregnant females of all species, and Barb was no exception. As her pregnancy progressed, her allergies eased up and became tolerable. Nevertheless, it was still a long nine months.

True to form, her due date came and passed. Once more, she was uncomfortable waiting and wanting to get on with the delivery. A few days after the due date, Barb asked to have labor induced, but her doctor preferred to wait on the baby's timing a bit longer. On Barb's fifth overdue day, we were sitting at the dinner table when I casually mentioned that I was reading an article about the history of medications.

"Would you believe that in the old days, they used castor oil to induce labor?" I asked jokingly. "Yuck. That stuff causes violent diarrhea and cramps, which is why they still use it today before a lower GI series. But apparently it causes all smooth muscle fibers to contract, including the uterus."

It seemed like an innocent comment at the time. Little did I know we had castor oil in the medicine cabinet. An hour later, Barb had swallowed a dose.

"What are you doing?" I asked. "You're going to regret that in a few minutes."

"I don't care. I just want this over!" she exclaimed.

Sure enough, Barb spent significant parts of the next two hours in the bathroom. But no labor.

We went to bed that night, with Barb frustrated that she still had to wait longer. I fell asleep easily, but in what seemed a few minutes later, I was awakened by Barb shaking me violently.

"The baby is coming, *now*! We have to get to the hospital!" she urged.

I jumped out of bed and hurriedly dressed. As I did, I remembered something about castor oil. It does not induce labor immediately; it generally took three to four hours to affect the uterus. And the race was on.

I called Barb's parents who were on call to watch the boys. Brian and Todd were both sound asleep, so we left them, knowing Barb's parents would arrive soon. Barb was in obvious distress, so there was no point in waiting. However, true to form, by the time we arrived at the hospital ten minutes later, her contractions had eased momentarily. While I filled out paperwork, a nurse took Barb into a cubicle for an initial exam.

"I think you are just having back pain, Barb. It may not be real labor," deadpanned the nurse.

"*It's not back pain!*" seethed Barb. "*All* of my labors have been like this!"

"OK. Just relax," the nurse responded reassuringly. "We're here to help. I'm going to do a pelvic exam."

I continued to fill out paperwork only to hear the nurse again two minutes later.

"Oh, my goodness! She's dilated eight centimeters. Call the doctor right away! He may not make it to this one. Take her straight to the delivery room."

The next thing I knew, Barb went whizzing by on a gurney, with her huge belly pointed skyward. I could see my third chance to witness the birth of one of our children disappearing into an elevator. And all because of a foolish comment at the dinner table about castor oil.

I scribbled illegible words in the final few blanks on the paperwork and threw them at the receptionist.

"Call upstairs, and let them know I'm on my way," I shouted over my shoulder. "I have to make it to this delivery!"

I could feel the receptionist shaking her head about another absurdly emotional father-to-be as I dashed toward the elevator. When I arrived in the delivery wing, one of the nurses saw me coming and pointed to a door.

"Your wife is already in delivery. The father's changing room is right through that door. Put on some scrubs, a mask, and a cap, and get in there as soon as you can."

I dashed into the room.

"Hold on, Barb. Try not to push," said a voice drifting in from the delivery room. "They just called and said your doctor has arrived and is headed upstairs. Hang on, and this will all be over in a few minutes."

I looked at the scrubs on the shelf. The space marked extra-large scrubs on the shelf was empty. Always fighting weight problems, I had a set of my scrubs in the trunk of the car for this very moment but, of course, I had totally forgotten them due to the urgency of the situation. If I headed for the car, it would certainly be all over before I returned. If I stuck my head out the door and asked for some extra-large scrubs, it probably would be too late as well. It was time for action, to hell with the consequences. I grabbed a pair of the green scrub pants marked size large, and I pulled them on. They stopped momentarily just past my knees, but I was committed, and I just kept pulling. I could feel most of the stitching in the inseam and crotch ripping free, but I somehow willed them to my waist. Next I grabbed a size large scrub top and repeated the process. Every seam in the arms and on the sides crackled as the stitching began to stretch and groan. Somehow I managed to get it on, but the arms were so tight, I could only raise them partway. It was almost impossible to tie on a cap and a mask, but it didn't matter. Somehow I managed, and I was going in.

As I dashed for the door to the delivery room, I passed a full-length mirror. Stuffed tightly in hospital green, I hoped to look something like the Incredible Hulk breaking out of my civilian clothes. However, the reality was that I looked far more like a St. Patrick's Day version of the Pillsbury Doughboy partially tethered in a straight jacket. It didn't matter. I was committed. Turning back was not an option.

Fortunately, as I entered the room, the doctor was coming through the door on the other side from the employees' scrub room. All eyes were focused on the doctor and Barb, and no one noticed the green creature that had just waddled in from the father's changing room. I sat down on a stool at Barb's end of the delivery table. More accurately, I leaned against the stool as the tight pants would not allow me to sit. I held Barb's hand. I could barely feel her hand as the tight scrub top was cutting off most of the circulation in my arms. But it didn't matter; I was there, *finally*! Scott David joined our family four minutes later. And most importantly, he and Barb were both doing better than I was in my straight jacket. I managed to give Barb a well-deserved kiss, all the while hoping my eyeballs would remain in their sockets. She had found relief, but I was still in pain.

Ten minutes later, as I peeled the remnants of the tattered scrubs off and tossed them into the laundry bin, I laughed at the thought of some unsuspecting worker discovering them later in the day. When Brian was born six years earlier, I had done my best to save $75. This time, I probably owed the hospital an extra $75 to cover the damage.

Once Barb and baby were settled and sleepy, I dashed home, delivered the news, showered, and headed for the office. It was a Thursday morning. Phil was out of town for the day. I was scheduled to work until noon. Red would be around and no doubt would offer to send me home and fill in for the morning.

I had just come out of the first office call of the morning, tired, with bags under my eyes. Red came down the hall in his signature coveralls crunching on his ever-present cigar.

"Congratulations! I hear you have another son," he said as he worked his jaws on the butt. "Good timing. You only need to see appointments until noon today. You can get some rest in this afternoon."

For the balance of the morning, I could see Red out of the exam-room window, training his ponies on a tether in the middle of the parking lot as always. He smiled and waved as each and every client drove in, still oblivious to how badly his ponies were congesting traffic. I shook my head, made one more mental note about how never to treat employees or clients, and motored on through the morning appointments.

"Just wait," said Cheryl noticing my gaze. "You haven't seen anything yet. The racing season starts soon, and he'll be out there with ponies harnessed to a chariot rather than just on a lunge line."

Chapter 24
Aruba
Lockport, Winter 1979

"HEY, PETE." IT WAS PHIL ON THE PHONE early one morning. "Sorry to dump a case on you, but I'm off to Aruba with Julie and have a dog I need you to look after. Her name is Sandy. She's a Cocker Spaniel owned by a nice family from Amherst. She has a long history of bad skin infections that usually respond to antibiotics. Two different vets in Amherst have treated the dog, but this recent bout of infection hasn't responded to oral antibiotics at all. The only thing I could suggest to the owners was to leave her with us for a few days to be treated with injectable antibiotics rather than oral meds. I set up a treatment schedule for the next few days, but feel free to change it to anything else if you have other thoughts. Watch your fingers—she's a bit nippy. I already warned Cheryl to get Ben's help when giving the injections."

"No problem, Phil," I responded. "We'll look after the dog. You and Julie have a great time in Aruba. I want to hear all about it when you get back. See you in ten days."

I reviewed the medical records that Sandy's family brought in from the other veterinary practices, and I agreed with Phil's course of action. Three days later, however, Sandy was no better, and I was perplexed. Both Cheryl and Ben were helping to hold Sandy as I examined her once again.

"You know what. I have this weird rash on both arms ever since this dog came in," Cheryl noted. "I must be allergic to something about this dog."

"That's weird," said Ben. "I have a rash on my arms and stomach. And I'm never sensitive to anything."

"Hold on a minute," I said as a lightbulb flashed brightly in my head. "That's too much of a coincidence. This dog doesn't have any classic lesions for sarcoptic mange, like crusty ears or reddened elbows, but we'd better check it out," I said. "Let's do a skin scraping to see if we find anything."

As I prepped and scraped away at a small patch of skin, Cheryl was asking questions.

"Wouldn't that be awful fast for sarcoptic mange to spread?"

"You're right," I responded. "And most of the time we see it in the summer, spread by foxes or coyotes. But every now and again, dogs can pick up the human form of scabies, which is another name for sarcoptic mange, especially if there are young children in the house that might have contracted scabies at day care or school. The human form is less common, but it's more likely to show up in the winter when all the kids are in school passing various diseases around. Check this slide out under the microscope, and let me know if you find anything.

"Great, I've got mange!" Cheryl shrieked from the lab five minutes later. "Doc, come check this slide out and tell me if I'm right."

"Yep, that's a scabies mite," I muttered as I peered into the eyepiece. "Don't panic. It's difficult to diagnosis, but it's easy to treat once you make the connection. Call your physician's office. Tell them you were exposed to a case of scabies. Be sure to call it scabies. Sarcoptic mange is more a veterinary term, and they might not recognize it. Your doctor might want to see you, or perhaps they will just call in a prescription for Quell. It's a shampoo that you apply in the shower, let sit for five minutes, and then rinse off. Tell Bob to do the same. That's the good news. The bad news is that Sandy needs to start on lime-sulfur dips as soon as possible. That's the best treatment for a dog with as many skin lesions as she has."

"Wonderful! I hate that stuff," Cheryl said as she wrinkled her nose. "The entire hospital smells like rotten eggs when we use it."

I headed for the phone to give Sandy's owners the same advice. They had several young children in the family, and it turned out that everyone in the household was itching. They too assumed they had all become sensitive to whatever was bothering Sandy. By the time I hung up the phone, the smell of rotten eggs was starting to invade the hospital. Three days later, after a second lime-sulfur dip repermeated the office with odor, Sandy went home. She was doing much better, as were Cheryl, Bob, and all the human members of Sandy's household.

A week later Phil returned to work.

"Hey Phil, glad to have you back. How was Aruba?" I asked.

"It's a great place!" Phil said. "Very hot, dry, and always windy. For the most part, we loved the trip. Only one problem. We both absolutely love sunny places, and I've never been prone to sunburn in the past. This time it looks like I got a bad case of sunstroke. Check this out," Phil said lifting his shirt to expose a bright red abdomen peppered with ugly blisters.

"Guess what Phil? That's not sunstroke. Do me a favor. Tuck in your shirt and don't get any closer," I requested. "Remember that Cocker you admitted just before leaving? We need to talk about her ..."

Phil's case of scabies was far worse than everyone else's, thanks to the heat of Aruba. Several hours later, he was in the shower treating his lesions.

CHAPTER 25
Picking a Location
Spring 1979

PHIL AND I HAD BECOME INTRIGUED by the demographic statistics that were so favorable for the success of a veterinary practice in the Buffalo area. Statistically speaking, the border area between Cheektowaga and West Seneca appeared to be the best spot for a new clinic. So we drove around, looking for a potential location. We located a vacant building that had once housed a convenience store on French Road, which divides the two townships. It seemed like a perfect location, so I made a call to see if the building was available for lease. It was, and the price seemed reasonable. The location was only five miles from Dr. Tom's clinic, so I had fairly good knowledge of the neighborhood and the type of clientele it would serve. The next step was to check with the town of Cheektowaga to make sure the property was properly zoned. Most suburban townships had their regulations worded vaguely for veterinary facilities. Basically, the zoning department supervisors could say yes or no depending on how you approached them and whether or not they felt your proposed facility would be an asset to the community.

"As you can see on these charts, the townships of Cheektowaga and West Seneca represent the best location for a new veterinary clinic," I said proudly, handing copies of our studies to the person in charge. "Demographic studies like these are the wave of the future. As you probably know, companies like McDonald's now use population and traffic demographics exclusively to pick new locations."

"That's impressive," responded the building supervisor. "Unfortunately, that particular building is not zoned favorably for a veterinary clinic. You would need a zoning variance, which would be virtually impossible."

I did my best to explain what a great asset a successful veterinary clinic would be in that location. Nonetheless, the request was turned down cold. Phil and I gave up on the location, and we began to look elsewhere. That turned out to be my first lesson in suburban town politics.

Six months later, another established Buffalo area veterinarian opened a second location in the very building we had targeted. Astonished, I asked a few colleagues about the situation. Apparently, the building supervisor or someone else high up in the town government was the father-in-law of the veterinarian. It seemed my dissertation about the demographic studies did impress someone well enough that he convinced his son-in-law to check things out.

After the Town of Cheektowaga turned down our request, we scouted around for other possible locations in that general area for a more favorable, commercially zoned location in either township. Nothing suitable surfaced. So it was back to the drawing board. Ironically, the Town of Tonawanda area and the area of Red's practice were both excellent locations, pretty much tied for second place based on our demographic studies. Since Phil and I were already established at Red's practice and both of us were gaining a favorable following from clients, we approached Red, and we let him know that we had an interest in purchasing the practice outright. We also made it clear to him that we did not want to go into a partnership with him. Red told us he was interested in a possible sale, so we authorized our management consultant to appraise the practice to establish a purchase price that was fair to both sides. We requested he send the business tax records to our consultant, and we waited for some indication that Red was serious. But days became weeks and weeks became months. It appeared that Red was doing everything possible to stall.

Finally, Phil and I decided to resume our search, this time focusing on the Town of Tonawanda. There was a very small storefront space available at the intersection of Brighton and Eggert roads.

"Its tiny, but this location is less than one block from where I grew up and where my parents live," I pointed out. "It's less than three blocks from where

Barb grew up and where her parents still live. And it's only two blocks from the high school we both attended. We have a lot of friends and connections in this neighborhood."

Even though the store itself seemed dramatically too small for a full-time practice, both of us were intrigued. While we were not optimistic about a purchase of Red's practice, we had not given up on the possibility. There was a new trend developing in veterinary medicine. Some of the larger practices in the country were establishing outpatient satellite clinics. These were small branches of the main hospital that offered basic services such as vaccinations and minor routine surgeries. Anything requiring hospitalization or a complex surgical procedure was referred back to the main hospital. Since the Tonawanda location was eighteen miles from Red's practice, the ideal situation would be for the Brighton and Eggert Road office to become a satellite clinic after Phil and I purchased Red's hospital. We realized, too, that if purchasing the Lockport practice did not work out, we would still have our own small office up and running.

Having just learned a valuable lesson in suburban town politics after losing the Cheektowaga location, we opted for a different approach. We decided to use our connections in the Town of Tonawanda. My father was a good friend of the town supervisor, and his connections had helped me land a summer job for the town parks department after my freshman undergraduate year. So I asked my father to make the initial contact with the town supervisor. Once again, we learned that the zoning of the location was such that the authorities could decide either for or against our proposal. This time, we received a green light to open the clinic.

"Both of our fathers think you guys are crazy locating there," Barb said one day. "But the small size means the rent will be low, so the risk isn't that bad. It would be great for the boys to be so close to both sets of grandparents. Let's go for it."

Phil and I put up few thousand dollars each for an initial budget. Barb and I had to borrow most of our share, and the planning began. We rented the storefront, and Barb came up with a simple design for a clinic. It had two small exam rooms, one of which would double as a surgery. In the middle, a very small reception area would also serve as a business office. One of the bathrooms was suitable for conversion to an X-ray developing darkroom for an ancient but serviceable portable X-ray unit we had targeted to purchase. The remainder of the space was for a small bank of cages and a dental sink that could also double as a treatment table. Finally, we hired a young carpenter to build the exam rooms, and we picked an opening date two months after our lease began.

CHAPTER 26

Opening Day
August 1, 1979

AS OUR OPENING DAY GREW CLOSER, so did the anticipation of our new adventure. Everything was falling into place. While the sign we had ordered for the building would not be ready by August 1, a temporary sign painted by a college art student was in the window, along with our new telephone number. Our basic drug inventory had arrived, as had some of our initial equipment. The remaining equipment was in transit and scheduled to arrive soon.

We had moved our family from Lockport to an apartment on Eggert Road very near the new office. An extension of the business phone was installed in our new home so that Barb could answer the phone whenever the office was closed, enabling us to schedule appointments without hiring staff. I would commute to Red's practice to continue employment there. Phil and I would see patients at the new office at times when we were not scheduled to work in Lockport. Red was less than pleased with our new plans. However, since Phil and I were handling almost the entire client load in his practice, he had little choice but to accept our decision.

The day before we opened, we learned that one important piece of equipment, our surgery table, would not arrive in time. We had one spay and two other appointments scheduled, and we were determined to stick to our commitments and schedule. Rather than delaying the first spay, Dad and I spent time late that night fashioning a temporary wooden platform that would fit on top of one of our desks and act as a surgery table for the time being.

We opened on a Wednesday, which was my day off at Red's clinic. We had hired Phil's fiancée, Julie, as our licensed technician, and she and I were the entire staff on that first day. The dog to be spayed was dropped off early in the morning so that we could do the surgery before the other patients arrived and so that the dog could recover and be ready to go home before we closed. Julie and I anesthetized the dog and prepped her for surgery. Soon the dog was strapped on her back on our temporary table, which was padded and covered with sterile drapes, ready for the first surgery in our new clinic.

As I lowered the scalpel blade and made the initial incision in the dog's abdomen, I knew that I was opening more than one dog's belly. I was opening the next chapter in my career and in my family's journey. Many of our friends and associates had questioned why Phil and I would open such a small office in a storefront building, but we were both confident. We were ready, and we would find a way to make it all work. As I opened the muscle layer in the dog, a smooth glistening surface appeared, and I began to laugh. It was my job to refresh Julie's technician skills, as she had been working in another field for the past two years. The one thing I had forgotten to remind her to do was to empty the dog's bladder. It took only a few minutes to work around the obstacle, and as I worked, I told Julie the story of my first day in surgery and the bladder I had inadvertently nicked on that day.

Soon I had removed the dog's ovaries and uterus, and I had begun to close the incision. I felt at peace, knowing that I was closing an incision and I was closing the first chapter of my career. I was closing an incredible ten-year journey that had led me from a high school science student to an experienced and capable veterinary surgeon. My life was no longer about "the making of a veterinarian." I was no longer questioning and vetting my own soul. I was an animal doctor. And once again, I was on top of the world.

An hour later, the dog was in her cage trying her best to wake up. She was looking up at us with glazed brown eyes struggling valiantly to wag her sleepy tail. I was installing new ceiling tiles in the back of the office, where the renovations were not yet complete. We had many little tasks to accomplish while we waited for the telephone to ring and our other appointments to arrive. There was lots of work to be done, and all of us were ready to do whatever it took to be successful.

An hour later, the telephone rang.

"Brighton-Eggert Animal Clinic, Julie speaking. Can I help you?"

"Hi," said the voice on the other end of the line. "I have an appointment with you for our cat's vaccinations in a few minutes, but I'm having trouble finding your office. I'm calling from a pay phone near the corner of Brighton and Eggert. Exactly where are you located?"

Julie looked out the front window, remembering there was a pay phone in our parking lot, twenty feet from our door.

"Turn to your right, and look through the window," she said to the woman. "I'm waving at you. Our sign hasn't arrived yet, but we're open. Come on in."

Less than a minute later, our client list had doubled.

CHAPTER 27
Exotic Pets
1980s

IT WAS NOT LONG AFTER the Brighton-Eggert Animal Clinic opened in August of 1979 that Dr. Phil Weber and I realized that it had the potential to be a full-time operation rather than just a satellite clinic. A new and serious disease in dogs, named Parvovirus, had been identified in 1978. Most veterinarians had seen and treated a few cases that year. However, toward the end of the summer in 1979, just after we opened our doors, the small number of cases erupted into a major epidemic that would continue for the next several years. Small animal veterinarians everywhere were working as many hours as they could to treat affected dogs. Some dogs recovered. Some did not. Before long, the first preventive vaccines became available, and the race was on to vaccinate dogs as quickly as possible to halt the epidemic.

Since Phil and I were working full time at Red's practice, we did not need a salary from our part-time endeavor. Our new business was successful enough that we were able to pay off the initial bills for our drugs and supplies by the end of our first six months of operation. We had no difficulty paying the lease payments on our basic equipment. At that point, we made the decision that it was time for me to cut back to twenty hours per week at Red's clinic to allocate more time to our new venture. Six months after that, I left Red's practice altogether to commit all of my time to Brighton-Eggert. After another six months, Phil was able to reduce his hours to twenty in Lockport to spend more of his time helping me care for our growing client base. Six months after that—two years after we opened—Phil left the Lockport practice altogether, and we both devoted all of our attention to our expanding young business.

Suddenly, we were doing something that seemed impossible. We were operating a full-time, two-doctor practice in 680 square feet of space with only two parking spaces. And it was one of the few practices in the country that had been started by two veterinarians rather than one. Because of the small office, for the most part, we could not both be in the building at the same time. We solved that by being open on multiple evenings and longer on Saturdays than most practices in the area. Since more and more households had both husband and wife in the workforce, the extended hours appealed to many people immediately. We operated that way for the next two years, with business ever increasing as much as it could given the limitations of our small location.

Yet despite the preponderance of sick dogs from the parvovirus epidemic, there were other animals to treat. In the early years, there were no exotic pet specialists in the Buffalo area, so we all did the best we could to help this special breed of pet owners. I have long maintained that the more exotic the pet, the more exotic the owner. In small animal medicine, any pet other than a dog or a cat is considered an exotic pet.

* * *

THE TURTLE

"Hi, Mr. Jenkins," I said. "I understand you have a pet turtle for us to examine today. Tell me a little about him."

"Doc, this is Pokey. We've had him for five years, and he's always been an active turtle. About a month ago, we started a major remodeling project at home, and we decided to move him to the basement for the winter months because of all the dust upstairs. About a week after we moved him, he developed a nasal discharge, and he became lethargic. I thought he'd be able to tolerate the cooler basement temperatures, but apparently it caused a bad infection."

"Well, I'm certainly not a turtle expert, but let's have a look," I said. "You're right. That's definitely a nasal discharge, so I agree that Pokey has a respiratory infection. We can probably help him out with that. There is a new antibiotic that we use in dogs and cats. I read an article recently that it's working well in turtles. Since turtles are cold-blooded and metabolize things slower than mammals, I'll give Pokey one injection in the muscles on the side of the tail. That should affect his blood levels for a good week. We can try that for the nasal discharge.

"However, I don't believe that the move to the basement was enough temperature change to cause an infection," I continued. "Perhaps the dust in the air from the remodeling started the respiratory symptoms. As for the lethargy, remember that turtles are cold-blooded, so the move to the basement would at least slow him down a bit. Also, and this is just a guess, if he's never been in a cooler location, Pokey's body may be getting a signal that it's time to hibernate. Has he ever hibernated before?"

"No. Do turtles hibernate?" Mr. Jenkins asked.

"It depends on where they live," I continued. "Turtles in the South generally don't hibernate. But here in the North, they bury themselves deep in the mud and sleep until the warm weather returns. Some owners put their turtles in the basement in the winter and give them a place to hibernate with the proper materials. I think most people just use dampened peat moss or wet shredded newspaper. You should stop at a library or a pet store and pick up a book on raising turtles. Pokey's problems could be much more serious than that, but my best guess is that he's just instinctively doing what turtles do. If you want, we can arrange for you to take him to see one of the specialists at the vet school in Ithaca."

"No, your theories sound reasonable," Mr. Jenkins responded. "Go ahead, Doc. Give him the injection. We can set something up in the basement for him to hibernate. Then we'll hope for the best."

Ten minutes later, I wrote up Pokey's medical chart. It read:

Turtle. Nasal Discharge. Lethargic. 1/2cc Gentocin injected in tail.
Turtle may be preparing to hibernate for the winter or forever.

"Hi Doc, you were right on the money," Mr. Jenkins reported via telephone in April. "Pokey was hibernating and is back to his normal crazy self the past couple of weeks."

THE RAT

"Hi, Mr. Cramer. I understand you have a pet rat you want us to examine. Tell me about your little gal," I urged.

"Well, Doc, this is Lumpy," Mr. Cramer said rather nervously. "She's a five-month-old rat with a large tumor on her side, and I'm sure it's bothering her quite a bit. Do you think you can remove the growth?"

The gray-colored rat with a hairless, raspy tail jumped out of the open door of its small cage into Mr. Cramer's cupped hands. She could have sat in one hand, but preferred to prance around happily despite a growth almost half her size. It was so big that it made her body tilt to the left.

"Wow, what a huge tumor. I've never seen anything quite like that!" I said, gently manipulating the mass with the tip of one finger.

"These guys are a bit tricky under anesthetic, but the growth doesn't feel like its invading the muscle below," I observed. "We may be able to remove it or at least try. But it's really large. I can't promise it won't re-form."

"That's great news, Doc," Mr. Cramer said, relaxing a bit but still a tad nervous. "I understand the risks, but I want to give it a try. Since you're willing to do the surgery, I need to come clean and tell you the rest of the story. Actually, I've seen many rats with tumors this size. You see—I work in the research department at the Roswell Park Cancer Institute downtown. We inject groups of young rats with cancer-causing agents. Then, after the tumors appear, the scientists try different drugs or chemicals to see if the growths shrink in size. When each experiment is over, the rats can't be used again, so we are supposed to humanely euthanize them. This particular rat had an incredible personality from day one. She got excited every time I came into the room. So, at the end of the experiment, I smuggled her out of the building in an old briefcase with a few small air holes cut into the side. I know it's strictly against the rules, but I'm hoping you'll understand."

"That's quite a story, Mr. Cramer," I said with a smile. "Many rats do have incredible personalities. As I'm sure you know, they often make better pets than hamsters or gerbils. But they just aren't popular because of their reputation for living in garbage and carrying disease," I said, watching the scientist's thick bushy eyebrows as they moved up and down above his black-framed eyeglasses.

"I know that the research rules for all lab animals are very strict," I continued. "Of course, those rules are for the protection of the animals to make sure that they are handled as humanely as possible while still conducting valuable research. I imagine that you have to deal with a lot of regulations. In any event, if this is the worst rule you ever violate in your life, I suspect you might still be eligible to get into Heaven," I said with a chuckle. "A contraband rat! That's certainly a first. But I'm certain Lumpy prefers your home to the alternative."

"Thanks, Doc, I appreciate that," Mr. Cramer said as he finally relaxed. "You're right. The rules are strict. We have to monitor how many times the air changes in the animal room each hour, and the Feds come in to check our logs every few months to make sure we follow all the rules. My office is right down the hall from the animal lab, but no one cares how many times the air turns over in my office," he laughed.

"Yep," I said. "But there is one big difference, isn't there?"

"What's that Doc?" he asked.

"You can open the window or leave your room whenever you want," I pointed out. "The rats don't have that option."

"Good point, Doc," he said with a smile. "I never thought about it that way. When can you do the surgery?"

"We can do it this morning," I offered. "Leave Lumpy with us and hope for the best. Plan to pick her up around two o'clock this afternoon."

Several hours later, the surgery was over, and Lumpy was about to head home.

"The surgery went pretty well. She handled the anesthetic without any problem," I assured Mr. Cramer. "I used buried absorbable sutures so that we won't need to worry about her chewing out the stitches. The incision looks good. You might need to think of a new name for her."

"No way, Doc!" he protested with his eyebrows rising above his glasses. "I've been calling her Lumpy since the growth first appeared. She'll always be Lumpy to me."

"You know what, Mr. Cramer?" I interjected. "I was thinking during the surgery how ironic it was for you to sneak her out of the building, carrying her past some of the best cancer surgeons in the country, only to bring her to me for surgery."

"I thought about that too, Doc. But there's a big difference," he said tilting his head toward me so that he could almost whisper. "All of those great surgeons would think I was just wacky, but you're a vet. You can understand."

"You've got a good point there, Mr. Cramer. Perhaps that means we're both just a tad crazy. I'm beginning to think there's no harm in that," I said with a wink.

"Thanks again, Doc. She looks much better now," he said as he pressed Lumpy's good side against his cheek with her teeth almost touching his nose. I smiled, shook my head a bit, and put my hand on his shoulder as he gently placed Lumpy back her small cage.

Mr. Cramer would be back with several more rats in the years to come.

The Rabbit

"Hi, Mr. and Mrs. Major. I understand your rabbit has a bad nasal infection. Tell me what's been happening," I inquired.

"Hi, Doc," volunteered Mrs. Major. "This is Fluffy, our one-year-old rabbit. Our kids are just crazy about her. About ten days ago, she developed a bad discharge from one nostril. We took her to Dr. Jones, and he prescribed these antibiotics. But they haven't helped, and we're very worried." She pulled an almost empty bottle of liquid antibiotics from her purse and placed it on the exam table.

"Hmm," I said examining the medication. "That's a good antibiotic for rabbits. Probably the same one I would have tried. Has the discharge always been from just one nostril? That seems strange."

"Yes," Mrs. Major said somewhat surprised. "Dr. Jones made the same comment."

"Well, let's get her out and take a look," I instructed.

148

Mrs. Major was a petite woman, likely just five feet tall. Mr. Major was a towering fellow, well over six feet tall, towering far above both his wife and my head as I sat on the exam room stool.

"Oh, my goodness! I see the problem. Nancy quick! Grab a mosquito forceps," I snapped as I nodded my head toward the appropriate drawer.

"What is it, Doc? Will she be OK?" asked Mrs. Major.

"This might be the weirdest thing I've ever seen," I suggested. "She'll be all right, but we probably will need to sedate her. There is a type of larva—a large, ugly maggot, actually called a cuterebra. We see them in late summer like this in rabbits and young kittens. There's a late-season fly that lays its eggs on the thin skin of rabbits, rodents, or young kittens. The eggs hatch and the larvae try to burrow through the skin. A large lump forms whenever a larva makes it under the skin. We know the lump has a cuterebra in it when a little nose with nostrils pops out of the opening for a second to breath. This one apparently got lost and became stuck in Fluffy's nostril."

As I spoke, Nancy handed me a tiny forceps, and then she held the rabbit firmly. I watched for the tiny nose of the grub to poke out of Fluffy's nostril once again. When it did, I made a quick stab and grabbed it with the hemostat. The rabbit went berserk, squirming and pulling backward despite Nancy's tight grip. A large, extremely ugly maggot came streaming out of the nostril. The rabbit shook its head, sneezed twice and settled down. I laid the maggot on a paper towel on the exam table and watched it slowly expand to about four times its previous diameter. In less than ten seconds it was as thick as my index finger, with skin that sported brown-tipped ridges resembling armor.

"Now that was a lucky stab!" I said with a smile. "These grubs are normally about an inch long and a half inch in diameter in the middle. This dude was stuck in the nasal passage and couldn't expand. I thought for sure we would need to knock Fluffy out to remove this darn thing. Too bad I didn't stop to take photos. This would have been a great case to send in to one of the veterinary journals."

Suddenly realizing I had just done something rather gross that I would typically never attempt in front of a pet owner, I glanced up from my seat. I was worried it might have been too much for the delicate looking young woman. She was fine, staring excitedly at the cuterebra with twinkling eyes.

"Neat!" she said. "Can I touch it?"

But far above her, I could see Mr. Major's eyes flutter several times, and then his body drifted slowly backward. He looked like a giant tree the moment before a lumberjack yells, "*Tim-ber.*" I jumped up from the chair and grabbed both of his elbows just as he fell backward into the exam room wall. Slowly, I helped him slide down to the floor, out cold but uninjured.

"Nancy, grab the first aid kit! There should be smelling salts in there. And tell Barb we may need to call the paramedics," I barked out.

"Relax, Doc, that's not the first time he's passed out," Mrs. Major said with a chuckle. "He went out cold the first time our daughter vomited. That's the easiest he's ever hit the ground. I'm not very good at catching him, as you can imagine. As they say, 'The bigger they are, the harder they fall.' That grub is really cool! Will Fluffy be OK?"

"Yep. I'm pretty sure she'll be fine," I responded while focused on her husband. "Are you sure we shouldn't call the paramedics?"

Just then Mr. Major shook his head and struggled to open his eyes.

"The rabbit," he mumbled looking up at the table. "Is there anything you can do Doc? The kids love that darn rabbit."

"Your bunny is going to be fine, Mr. Major. Are you OK?" I asked while I discreetly wrapped the huge maggot in the paper towel and handed it to Nancy. I wanted to make sure it was totally out of sight before Mr. Major's eyes regained good focus.

Both patients made full recoveries and headed for home a few minutes later.

CHAPTER 28

Mrs. Kay

1980s & 1990s

LATE IN 1983, THE BUILDING ACROSS the street, a former Texaco gas station, went up for sale. We were doing well, but we were not yet in a position to buy the property in a conventional manner. Yet, at the same time, we could not afford to miss the opportunity to acquire the building. By that time I was more confident about my business skills, so I approached a number of attorneys until I found one who would assist us in negotiating a high-risk wraparound mortgage. We needed the building, so we accepted the risk involved, and we moved forward. By April of 1984, our initial remodeling of the former gas station was complete, and we moved across the street. Overnight we went from a hard-to-find storefront with insufficient parking to a highly visible property that cars could easily reach from either Brighton or Eggert Road. Better yet, we finally had ample parking. Business exploded. In a few short years the high-risk mortgage was paid off as new additions were financed in a more conventional and safer fashion.

* * *

"Doc, Mrs. Kay is on the phone, *again*. She has more questions about Shultz's diabetes. Line two," advised Marty, one of our receptionists.

"OK, No problem," I responded. "It's fun talking to her."

"Hi, Mrs. Kay. How is Shultz doing today?" I inquired.

"Oh, Doctor, *Doctor*, **Doctor!**" said Mrs. Kay in a voice that quivered. "I'm so glad to hear your voice. I'm *very* worried about Shultz. He only ate half of his meal this morning and drank less water than usual. He urinated well, but he only had a tiny bowel movement. We gave him his normal amount of insulin this morning. Was that OK? I'm very worried we did something wrong."

"No, that's OK" I said reassuringly. "Shultz will be fine, Mrs. Kay. As long as he ate some amount of food, it's all right to give him his morning insulin. Make sure he eats something tonight before you give him his evening injection. If he doesn't eat tonight, then just give him half his normal dosage, and call me in the morning."

"Oh, thank you, thank you, *thank you*, Doctor! I feel so much better after hearing the sound of your voice," she said in a voice that had calmed a bit.

I was never quite sure if Mrs. Kay or the family dog was my patient. Somehow it was fun to treat them both. Many of our most memorable long-term clients had been allowing us to treat their pets since our early days. Mrs. Kay was the quintessential example. She had called for a second opinion shortly after Shultz had been diagnosed with diabetes mellitus, or sugar diabetes, as she preferred to call it. She needed far more hand-holding than most clients. As a new practice, time was something we had in abundance, so I quickly became the Kay family veterinarian.

To say that Shultz, the Kay family Miniature Schnauzer, was a child substitute for Edna Kay would have been an understatement. Her life had been dedicated to children. She and her husband, James, had recently retired after entertaining children for a living, literally. They had produced puppet and marionette shows. James handled the puppets and marionettes while Edna provided the voices. They performed in front of live audiences and even had their own live local television show in the earliest days of television. They also had raised two children of their own, Karen and Jim. Both "kids" still lived at home. But they were young adults now, pursuing their own professional careers. The family dog was the only "child" left in Edna's life. And that dog was now the centerpiece of her world.

I generally talked to Mrs. Kay on the phone several times each week and occasionally multiple times in a day. I would see her and her dog at the office a couple of times each month. Generally, at least one other family member accompanied Mrs. Kay to the office. She was simply too emotional to go it alone without support. While all of the family members were incredibly devoted to the family pet, husband James, daughter Karen, and son Jim were typically able to stay on the proper side of reality.

Edna, on the other hand, made frequent short trips into the *Twilight Zone* of pet ownership. When that happened, it became my job to coax her back across the blurry line that defined reality. Whenever the family dog became ill enough to come to the office, she always assumed the worst and was convinced that I would deliver news that the dog was going to die. Usually, my voice on the phone brought her back into the rational world, but on those occasions when the family schnauzer was ill enough to come in, it frequently took more than my voice to reassure her. Once in the office, Mrs. Kay would be too nervous to sit down. She would shake with anxiety to the point where it was awkward for her to stand still. Her small frame was forced to pace in a room that was too small for pacing. Her aging, wrinkled skin seemed to ripple even worse when she worried.

Somehow I stumbled onto the realization that if I cracked a joke during the office call, her tears of fear could often be quickly converted into tears of joy. So I always used my amateur skills as a comedian every bit as much as my professional skills as a veterinarian when examining the Kay family dog.

Since Shultz was already older and diabetic when Brighton-Eggert opened, it wasn't long before his health declined, and he passed on. Naturally, that was an extremely difficult time for Edna Kay, but she had excellent family support to help her through the process. I encouraged the entire family to take their time finding a new pet. Rushing out to buy the first puppy available was not the way to go.

Despite my recommendation, Mrs. Kay, with Karen and Jim in tow, were back in the office in less a week with a new Miniature Schnauzer puppy, this one named Tootie. It was obvious in a flash that Tootie was going to be a rambunctious dog, far more work than Shultz had been. I rolled this eight-week-old puppy over in my hands and watched as she struggled and protested instantly. It's a very simple test for picking out a calm puppy, but very few people know how to do it. For a dog, lying on its back is submissive behavior. A calm puppy will allow you to roll it over and will generally grow to become a well-behaved adult. On the other hand, a puppy that is destined to be the aggressive alpha dog struggles vehemently and will not allow itself to be placed on its back, even at this young age. Tootie's reaction was not totally alpha, but it was clearly not submissive behavior, alerting me from day one that she was destined to be a "problem child." Of course, by the time any pet owner brought a new puppy to the office, it was already too late to teach them this simple trick. They had already become attached to the puppy they selected and would never consider turning back.

By the time Tootie turned a year of age, she had become a little devil. Like so many assertive dogs, she had the Kay household rather well trained. Tootie's biggest problem trait was her tendency to eat virtually anything that happened to drop onto the floor. Tootie was only an appropriate name if you considered the gas she passed after eating things a dog was never designed to eat. And it didn't matter if the object was animal, vegetable, or mineral, Tootie ate it. She was a canine vacuum cleaner. She should have been named Hoover, Eureka, or better yet, Dirt Devil.

Most of Tootie's adventurous eating caused only minor problems, but occasionally it caused both her and the Kays enough distress that it was necessary to bring her to the clinic for evaluation and treatment. Most veterinarians label the GI symptoms caused by this type of behavior to be the result of "dietary indiscretion." However, I was never comfortable with that term. To me dietary indiscretion more aptly described why I and so many others fought the battle of the bulge year after year. So I had long ago coined my own more pseudo-medical term—*garbagitis*. Tootie visited the clinic often on a monthly basis with bouts of garbagitis, and I treated her with the magic of injections designed to control vomiting and diarrhea. At the same time, I treated Mrs. Kay's anxiety with the tone of my voice and with my amateur wisecracks.

At times, when Tootie was highly distressed by the GI symptoms from a particular bout of garbagitis, she became a bit snappy at home, where she knew full well that she was the boss. In the office, she was rarely if ever, a problem to handle. On one particular occasion, Tootie had behaved very poorly at home prior to her appointment, so Mrs. Kay assumed the worst and expected her to bite either the assistant or me.

"Doctor, *Doctor*, please use a muzzle," she pleaded. "I'm so afraid she is going to bite someone. Please, please, *please*, use a muzzle."

I had a new assistant, Susie, in the room that day. She had only been on our staff for a little over a week, so she didn't know Tootie, the Kay family, or any of the idiosyncrasies so well known to the rest of the staff. Yet she had worked for a veterinary clinic for many years before she moved to Buffalo and joined our staff. I was confident she could restrain Tootie without any need for a muzzle.

"Please, Doctor, *please*, use a muzzle," Mrs. Kay repeated again and again.

"I would love to use a muzzle," I deadpanned in the middle of the exam without looking up. "Unfortunately, we simply don't have one that would fit *you*."

In my peripheral vision, I could see Jim and Karen trying to resist the temptation to laugh out loud. And I could see and hear Mrs. Kay quivering, too, vibrating from laughter. But the poor new employee was only facing me and could see none of this. Her eyes dilated like a deer in the headlights of a car at night, as she assumed I had just rudely and needlessly insulted a pet owner. Five minutes later, Tootie was pulling on her leash, anxious to take her family home to the place where she was truly the boss. And a few of our employees were chatting in the hallway, explaining the entire Kay family history to the newest member of our Brighton-Eggert family of employees.

On another occasion, however, Tootie's bad habit did cause a close encounter with the Grim Reaper. Tootie had vacuumed a stray penny off the kitchen floor. Even though Edna Kay saw Tootie inhale the penny, picked her up, and virtually ran her to the clinic, an X-ray confirmed that the penny had already exited the stomach and had entered the small intestines.

"Oh *no*! What does that mean, Doctor? Is she going to die?" she asked in a panic.

"Well Mrs. Kay, it's already too late to induce vomiting," I said pointing to the penny on the X-ray. "And it's important that the penny keep moving forward. If it does, it should pass in three or four days. But if it stops moving, we'll need to do surgery immediately to remove it. Bring her back tomorrow at about the same time, and we'll take another X-ray."

Everything I told Mrs. Kay was the truth. But there was a lot of the truth that I had decided to leave out. Since I knew that one of my jobs was to be Mrs. Kay's unlicensed psychologist, I had decided not to torment her with the rest of the story. Only if surgery became necessary would I reveal my deepest fears. If the penny kept moving, I could avoid the issue.

Prior to 1983, pennies were minted out of high-grade copper. Those pennies caused little harm as copper does not break down rapidly in the GI track and cause toxic reactions. In 1983, however, when the price of minting a penny out of copper exceeded one cent, the government changed the alloy to mostly zinc. And the zinc in those pennies can cause major problems. Zinc dissolves more easily in the digestive track, and if too much zinc is absorbed, an irreversible toxic reaction could shut down the kidneys and the pancreas. And the condition was almost always fatal. There was no way to determine the date of the penny that Tootie had swallowed, and there was a fifty-fifty chance that this was a dangerous one. I needed to get that coin out one way or another in five days or fewer. If I didn't, Tootie, the Kay family, and I could all be swept into the real *Twilight Zone* of veterinary medicine.

Each day, Mrs. Kay arrived at the clinic with Tootie and at least one family member for moral support. We would take Tootie in the back and take an X-ray. Even though the films revealed that the penny was moving, Mrs. Kay became more and more frightened each and every day. And so did I. On day four, the X-ray showed that the penny had passed the most critical point. It had moved out of the small intestine and into the large bowel. But I knew my window of opportunity to get the penny out without surgery was closing, regardless of the progress. So rather than send Tootie back home for another twenty-four hour vigil, I instructed the technicians to give her an enema and put her in a kennel run for a few minutes. Thankfully, the indignity of the procedure encouraged the dog to move her bowels quickly, and the penny came out. The technicians retrieved the penny, washed it up, and gave it to me in a sealed plastic baggie to present to the Kay family. It was a dangerous, zinc-laden penny.

I walked back into the exam room with Tootie on a leash in one hand

and a plastic baggie with the shiny penny polished by digestive enzymes in the other. I sported a smile that stretched from ear to ear. Mrs. Kay lost total control of her emotions. She threw her arms around me and sobbed loudly.

"Oh thank you, thank you, *thank you*! Doctor," she said as the quivering of her diminutive body sent waves through my large frame.

"But, *but*, What, *what* would have happened if she had swallowed a nickel rather than a penny?" she asked weeping profusely.

"Well, Mrs. Kay," I said as I winked at Karen and Jim standing behind her, "we would have gotten the nickel out, but let's be thankful it wasn't a nickel. I would have had to charge you five times as much for a nickel!"

Karen and Jim exploded in laughter. And the tears that were slowly rolling down Edna Kay's face seemed to dance faster and faster as they hopped from wrinkle to wrinkle. Almost instantly her mood was converted into sobs of joy.

Tootie ignored all of this. She simply wagged her little stump of a tail, pulled on the leash, and sniffed as hard as she could under the exam room door. She could smell the freedom of the outside world, where she was in control.

CHAPTER 29
Gigi
1990s

SOON, DR. PHIL AND I WERE DISCUSSING THE next logical step for the clinic—hiring associate veterinarians. We got along well but were concerned about adding additional personalities to the mix. Might it mess up the excellent chemistry we shared? But the business was growing so rapidly that we decided to take the next step. From that point on, to keep pace with the growth, we added a new veterinarian every second or third year and added a new addition to the building every third or fourth year.

Not long after moving into our new building, Barb began working full time for the practice, slowly handling more and more of the management. At some point in time, I came to the realization that I really enjoyed long-term planning, both on a medical and business level, while Barb's strongest talents were in the very areas I was weakest—day-to-day scheduling, payroll, and bookkeeping. As a result, I finally made the move that is perhaps the hardest for start-up business owners—letting go and delegating responsibility to others. I turned the drug and supply ordering over to our head technician, and I empowered Barb to oversee all of the day-to-day management. The business continued its expansion beyond anyone's expectations.

By 1998 we had added four additions to the initial building. We had a staff of eight veterinarians, and our growth continued. By that time, the Brighton-Eggert Animal Clinic was being used as a model by the same practice-management consultant that had helped us choose a location back in 1979. When the consultant gave lectures around the country or published articles, the charts and numbers were often our numbers, without revealing our name or location.

* * *

"Doc, Mr. Evans is in Room Two with Gigi," said Millie our receptionist. "She's in rough shape. She's an eleven-year-old poodle, and she hasn't been spayed. We tried all last week to get Mr. Evans to bring her in. It sounds like a pyometra, so we told Mr. Evans that she probably needs surgery. He yelled and swore at us on the phone claiming all he needed were pills to make her better. At least he finally brought her in. His wife passed away about eight months ago. She always cared for their pets."

"OK. Thanks," I responded. "Let's see what we've got."

As I examined Gigi, there was little doubt that the staff was correct in their concern that this was a pyometra—a severe infection of the uterus generally seen in older female dogs about two months after an estrus cycle. Gigi should have been treated days or even weeks ago. The medical record clearly indicated that we had recommended spaying Gigi many times over the years. There were notations indicating that Mrs. Evans wanted to spay the dog, but her husband always resisted.

"Mr. Evans, it's clear that Gigi has a life-threatening infection in her uterus," I stated. "The bacteria that cause this type of infection enter the uterus during the heat cycle, when the cervix is open. Then they become trapped inside when the cycle ends. They multiply and eventually secrete a toxin. That toxin has weakened Gigi's kidneys. That's why she's been drinking so much water. Her kidneys aren't able to concentrate the urine as they normally would. The infection is very advanced, and she is extremely weak. Her only chance is to have an immediate hysterectomy. I can't promise she will survive the surgery, and if she does, I can't promise her kidney function will return to normal. Medication absolutely will not help without surgery. It's either surgery or its time to make the decision to put her down."

"No way, Doc. Do the surgery right away!" Mr. Evans said adamantly. "Gigi was my wife's favorite pet. I want to do everything possible to keep her going."

It was obvious Mr. Evans was among that small percentage of clients who display an abrasive personality when dealing with the front office staff, yet present a pleasant personality when dealing with one of the doctors.

Gigi was in surgery a few hours later and somehow managed to make it through the procedure despite her weakened condition. We kept her hospitalized for two days to support her with intravenous fluids and antibiotic injections. When her kidney values returned to normal, I decided to try sending her home, hoping that even though she showed almost no appetite, being in familiar surroundings would lift her spirits.

"You are going to need to be patient, Mr. Evans," I warned. "It could be a week or more until Gigi regains her strength. Make sure that she drinks fluids and takes her antibiotics. Offer her tiny amounts of different foods, but don't be concerned if she doesn't eat much for the next few days."

Mr. Evans took Gigi home, but only four hours later, he was on the phone, screaming and swearing at one of our receptionists. He was certain we had wasted his money recommending surgery since Gigi was listless and had no appetite. One of the technicians got on the phone and reiterated everything I had told him just hours before.

"Doc, we have a problem," Mille said the next day. "Mr. Evans is out front swearing up a storm in the waiting room. He is insisting that we put Gigi down to end her suffering."

"OK. Park him in an empty room, and I'll have a chat with him." This time, I could hear the foul language drifting from the waiting area.

After a brief exam, I assured Mr. Evans that Gigi was doing as well as could be expected and that she needed a few more days to recover her strength and appetite. Mr. Evans refrained from using inappropriate language in my presence, but he adamantly insisted that we euthanize Gigi.

"Mr. Evans, the decision is ultimately yours, but you *are* making the wrong decision," I finally said after going back and forth for several minutes. "I would have understood if you had opted to put Gigi down rather than subject her to surgery. However, now that she's had the surgery, she deserves every chance to recover. We will *not* put her down at this clinic at this time.

If you are that insistent, I can only recommend that you take her over to the SPCA and have her put down there."

I felt there was at least a slim chance that if someone elsewhere encouraged him to wait a bit longer, he might accept his or her advice.

Mr. Evans scooped Gigi off the exam table and stormed out, making sure to slam the exam room door loudly behind him. I could hear more foul language directed to the front desk as he headed out the exit.

Understanding their emotional struggle, we always tried to give clients as much leeway as possible when their animals were severely ill. However, I sensed this was one of those incredibly rare moments when I needed to "fire" a client for the sake of our staff. All of the employees simply cared too much and tried too hard to be subjected to repeated insults from this type of pet owner.

Several hours later I wrote a letter to Mr. Evans. I thanked him for the business he had brought to our clinic over the years, and then I wrote that I regretted to inform him that we would no longer be able to provide veterinary services to any of his pets. I noted that it was obvious that he no longer had faith in our recommendations, and that he had insulted our staff with his abusive tirades. I closed the letter by stating that it was far better for him to be a happy client at some other veterinary office than an unhappy client at our facility. After attaching a copy of the medical records for all of Mr. Evans pets as well as a copy of a directory of all other veterinary clinics in the area, I put the letter in the outgoing mail.

A couple of months later, the receptionist came looking for me.

"Doc, we have a problem. Remember Gigi's owner, Mr. Evans? He's out in the waiting room almost begging to come back as a client. He is being extremely polite, and we're getting really strange looks from the other pet owners in the waiting room."

"OK." I groaned. "Park him in an exam room. I'll have a chat with him in a couple of minutes when I finish the last few sutures on this laceration."

We had never taken back a client that had been fired, and I had no intention of changing that now.

"Hi, Mr. Evans. Please have a seat. What brings you here today?" I asked.

Mr. Evans sat in a chair but could not look at me. He stared at the floor.

"I was hoping you would take me back as a client," he said as he pulled a Polaroid snapshot out of his shirt pocket and laid it on the table.

"That looks like a nice photo of Gigi," I said. "How long before she died did you take this photo?"

"I took it yesterday, Doc," Mr. Evans muttered, still unable to look up. "When I left that day, I drove over to the SPCA, and I sat in the parking lot for a few minutes trying to say good-bye. But all I could remember was how much my wife enjoyed going there to look at the pets that were up for adoption. She even volunteered at the shelter a few times over the years. Billy, one of our cats, was adopted there. Eventually, I decided to take Gigi home for one more night. The next day she started eating, and she's been great ever since. By the time the stitches were ready to come out, she was acting like a puppy again. I took her to that clinic over on Delaware Avenue since your letter told me not to come back here. But I didn't like the place. All of the employees there seemed so cold, and it made me understand how rude I'd been here. I decided to stop by to see if there was any way we could start over again."

"Well, I'm glad Gigi did fine and that you still have each other," I said exhaling deeply. "I understand how someone's emotions can get the best of them when they feel their pet is dying. But, unfortunately, I can't tolerate a client who yells and swears at our staff. They try too hard to help, and they deserve better treatment."

"I know, Doc," he said still looking at the floor. "My wife always got as mad as can be when I used foul language."

"I'll tell you what." I replied. "I've never done this before, but I think we will take you back as a client, but only on probation. Any foul language and we will have to part company once again and permanently."

Mr. Evans started to choke up, and tears dripped from the corners of his eyes.

"My wife always used that term," he sniffled. "She always told me she was placing me on probation when she got mad at me."

"I'll bet it wasn't the pets that she was threatening to withhold, was it?" I asked with a smile.

"You're right about that, Doc. You must be married," he replied.

"Twenty-four years, Mr. Evans," I said. "Twenty-four wonderful years."

"Thanks, Doc. My wife would be so mad at me right now," he said finally looking up.

"No, she wouldn't," I said shaking my head. "She would have been mad as a hatter when you wanted to put Gigi down. But she would have been proud as heck of you ever since you left the SPCA parking lot and took her home. Now go home, and give this cute little dog a hug from your wife," I instructed slipping the photograph back in his shirt pocket.

Mr. Evans was never a problem again, and I was ever more cautious about firing clients than I had been in the past.

CHAPTER 30

Terry Anderson's Dog
More Dr. Phil

DR. PHIL WEBER'S ROLE IN THE GROWTH of Brighton-Eggert and its success over the years cannot be overstated. Any description of my personal journey through time would not be complete without a bit more about Phil.

* * *

In 1985, Terry Anderson, a journalist working for the Associated Press, was taken hostage in Beirut, Lebanon, and held for over six years. During that time, a dog owned by Terry ended up at the Brighton-Eggert Animal Clinic in need of emergency surgery. The dog was a purebred Rhodesian Ridgeback.

It was our understanding Terry had been on assignment in South Africa prior to his travels as a journalist to Lebanon. Apparently, he had acquired the dog in Africa and brought it home to the United States. When Terry accepted his next overseas assignment, he arranged to leave the dog with his sister, Peggy Say, who lived in the nearby village of Batavia. However, as time dragged on, Peggy became discouraged at the lack of progress in obtaining her brother's freedom. She became politically active and was in the news frequently, working to keep the memory of Terry's captivity alive. She often traveled to Washington to try her best to keep the U.S. government focused on his plight. Due to her travels, she needed to place the dog with someone else and chose a close friend who lived just a few blocks from our clinic.

Unfortunately, the dog developed a gastric torsion, one of the worst possible emergencies seen in larger dogs. Essentially, the stomach flips over inside the abdominal cavity and twists on itself, cutting off both the circulation of blood and the ability of food, liquids, and gas from exiting the stomach in either direction. This condition often leads to a condition sometimes called bloat because of the rapid accumulation of gas trapped in the stomach. It often leads to a quick and very painful death. Veterinarians generally recommend that large-breed dogs be fed in split meals rather than once daily and never be allowed to exercise immediately after eating to minimize the risk of gastric torsion.

Fortunately, the caretaker for Terry's dog realized that something was seriously wrong and brought the dog to our clinic quickly. Within minutes of arrival, X-rays were taken and treatment was initiated. While Dr. Phil worked on the dog, our receptionists helped the dog's caretaker to contact the Associated Press headquarters in New York City for guidance. They agreed to cover any costs necessary for the dog, up to and including surgery if necessary. Unfortunately, the dog required emergency surgery since the torsion could not be untwisted without surgical intervention.

As an extremely skilled surgeon, Phil quickly had the problem corrected. In surgery the excess gas was deflated, the stomach was untwisted, and finally a portion of the organ was sutured to the lining of the abdomen to decrease the likelihood of torsion in the future. The dog began to show immediate improvement and was out of surgery in less than two hours. However, these are difficult cases to manage for the first day after surgery. Everything is touch and go for a while, even with a good surgical correction.

As the day went on, the clinic began to receive multiple telephone inquiries from various representatives of the Associated Press checking on the progress of the dog. Some of the calls were from AP staffers who knew Terry. A couple of the inquiries were from nationally recognized news correspondents. Phil fielded every call himself rather than relaying messages through any of the technicians or receptionists.

Gradually, the dog did better and better. Phil, on the other hand, did worse and worse, thanks to the incoming calls. Rather than being his normal, confident self, he worried more and more about possible postoperative complications along with a potential for negative publicity should anything go wrong. That evening he sent Julie home to retrieve a sleeping bag, and he slept on the hard ceramic tile floor in front of the dog's kennel that first night after surgery.

The next morning, the dog was doing fine, but Phil looked haggard.

"How comfortable were you last night?" I asked.

"More comfortable than Terry," was Phil's only response.

The dog made an uneventful, complete recovery from surgery and went home shortly thereafter.

Terry Anderson eventually was freed in 1991 and returned home with the unfortunate distinction of being the longest-held hostage in United States history. During his confinement, Terry renewed his faith in Christianity and wrote many poems that were published after his return. Perhaps he wrote one of those poems as Dr. Phil Weber slept next to his dog.

CHAPTER 31

Molson's Secret
More Dr. Phil

"HI, DOCTOR PHIL. GEORGE AND I ARE worried about Molson today," said Mrs. Jenkins as Phil began to examine his next patient. "He's always eats strange things and then vomits them up a few hours later. But now he hasn't eaten in three days, and he's vomiting on and off. He seems lifeless and won't even drink water."

Molson was a Golden Retriever about two years old, and the Jenkins seemed like both the perfect couple and excellent pet owners. They brought Molson into the clinic often, and they always followed our advice without question.

"Hmm! That doesn't sound very good," Phil warned. "Let's have a look."

A few minutes later, he finished his exam.

"Molson has a fever, a lot of abdominal pain, and the whites of his eyes are bloodshot. That's not good news," he reported. "If he swallowed something, he may need surgery. Leave him with us, and I'll call you as soon as we get some X-rays and blood work done. Any idea what he might have eaten?"

"Not a clue, Dr. Phil. We both racked our brains, but nothing seems to be missing," said Mr. Jenkins. Mrs. Jenkins nodded in agreement.

An hour later, Phil was on the phone with Mrs. Jenkins.

"I'm afraid your fears were correct," Phil said. "The X-rays show a blockage in Molson's intestinal track, and his white blood count is quite elevated. We need to get him into surgery right away."

"Go ahead, Dr. Phil," she responded. "Please call us as soon as you finish.

Do whatever you need to do. Molson is like our child."

"We all know that, Mrs. Jenkins," Phil said reassuringly. "Don't worry. We'll do everything we can to get him through this. I'll be in touch."

Two hours later, Phil had Molson's abdomen open on the surgery table and a portion of his intestines exposed. He had located a large lump in the middle of his small intestine, and he made a small opening. He extracted a clump of some type of lightweight cloth all covered with digestive track contents. He dropped the clump of cloth into a surgical pan.

"Fortunately, there doesn't seem to be any damage to the intestines," he said. "I won't need to remove any sections of bowel. You know the drill, Heather. Rinse that thing out. The Jenkins will want to know what Molson ate if we can figure it out."

Less than an hour later, two assistants were carrying Molson out of surgery on a stretcher headed toward recovery. Dr. Phil was removing his gloves.

"Take a look at this!" Heather said, giggling. "It looks like Molson was upset that the Jenkins were paying attention to something other than him!"

Heather held up a large plastic bag. The digestive process had faded the contents of the bag. However it was obviously a very sexy piece of woman's lingerie, a pair of very scanty panties. On the small elastic waistband the words "Victoria's Secret" were faded but still visible.

"Oh boy," Phil muttered. "This is going to be interesting. I'll give the Jenkins a call and try to pass on the news without embarrassing them."

Fifteen minutes later Mrs. Jenkins answered the phone.

"The surgery is done, and I'm optimistic Molson will be fine," he said. "We were able to remove the foreign object, and none of the intestines were permanently damaged."

"That's great news Dr. Phil. What did you find?" she inquired.

"Well," Phil said hesitating a bit. "The techs are still cleaning it up, but it looks like it's probably a pair of women's underwear," he added, trying to be as diplomatic as possible.

"Oh great! That's just what I need," she moaned. "I'm always yelling at George for leaving his clothes lying around on the floor. I'm never going to hear the end of this one."

"Don't worry. These things happen," Phil responded. "Retrievers who eat things are prone to do it again. So it's going to be important for both of you to keep things cleaned up in the future. And it sounds like that will probably be easier for you than for your husband."

"When do you think Molson can come home?" Mrs. Jenkins asked.

"We always monitor this type of surgery here in the hospital the first night. Tomorrow, if his temperature is normal, we'll start with a small amount of water and then go from there. If everything goes well, Molson may be ready to go home tomorrow evening."

"Good. I hope it works out that way," she said. "George is working tomorrow night, so I can pick him up alone."

The next evening, Molson was doing well and ready for discharge. Some of the employees were speculating as to whether or not Mrs. Jenkins had told her husband the whole truth about what was removed during the surgery. Dr. Phil went into the room with Mrs. Jenkins, reviewed the X-rays, explained the post-op instructions, and reunited her with Molson. When he finished, Mrs. Jenkins asked if the clinic had saved the underwear. Phil had the plastic bag with the scanty panties inside Molson's medical folder.

"Sure, we always try to do that whenever possible."

He reached into the folder, extracted the bag, and laid it on the exam table as Mrs. Jenkins was hugging Molson. In an attempt to minimize a potentially embarrassing moment, Phil swiveled his medical stool around and opened Molson's folder on the counter behind him. He pretended to review all the medical entries to allow Mrs. Jenkins a moment of privacy to get over any embarrassment.

"THAT BASTARD!" Mrs. Jenkins screamed out, loud enough to be heard two exam rooms away. "That bastard," she repeated, this time barely audible as her face was buried in Molson's hair muffling both her words and her tears.

"I … I don't understand," Dr. Phil said apologetically as he turned back to look at Mrs. Jenkins and Molson. "Is something wrong?"

"Those aren't mine," she said softly with her face still buried in Molson's fur. "I've suspected something was going on for the last few months. There were a lot of little signs, including Molson's behavior. But I never ever expected that bastard would cheat on me in our own home."

"Oh dear. I'm so sorry," Phil said. "Are you sure? We just assumed, well, I don't know what to say."

"You don't need to say anything, Dr. Phil. You guys have been great. And I've been in denial for a long time. In a way, it's going to be easier now knowing the truth rather than just wondering."

"Here," Phil said, handing Mrs. Jenkins the small box of Kleenex kept in each exam room for distraught pet owners.

"You and Molson need a few moments alone," he continued. "You can stay in this room as long as necessary to collect yourself. When you're ready to leave, come through this back door rather than going out into the waiting room. One of our employees will help you out the side door." It was a method of egress generally offered to owners after a pet's euthanasia.

Ten days later, Mrs. Jenkins was back with Molson to have his sutures removed. Both seemed to be recovering from their traumas. Mr. Jenkins, however, was never seen or heard from again.

* * *

One would expect a story like this to have been unique. However, I have heard variations on this theme three times during my three decades in practice. Two on them occurred in our clinic. Years after Molson's incident, a similar scenario unfolded at another Buffalo-area veterinary hospital. That incident was reported in one of the veterinary journals. We marveled at the incredible parallel of the cases.

Perhaps this has happened because dogs simply love to check out and chew on objects with unusual odors. Socks generally head the list of objects ingested, but undergarments are never far behind. In fact, over the years, dogs have often presented veterinary employees with many surprises. Most frequently this occurred on the morning of a scheduled surgery. Owners have always been instructed to withhold food overnight just as in human medicine. After admission to the hospital, patients are given pre-op medications that decrease the likelihood of anesthetic complications. If there is something in the stomach that does not belong, it is often vomited up shortly thereafter. A long list of unexpected presurgical offerings goes far beyond socks and underwear. Aluminum foil, pieces of plastic or rubber objects, rocks, bottle caps, batteries, jewelry, baby diapers, corn cobs, a morning feeding owners insist was not given, and endless other things round out that list. In the world of veterinary medicine, dull moments have always been in short supply.

* * *

By 1998, Dr. Phil Weber had turned 65 and had decided it was time to plan his retirement. We arranged for our management consultant to come into town one Wednesday to start mapping out his retirement. Unfortunately, the Lord had other plans, and Phil suffered a sudden and fatal brain aneurism on the Saturday night before that meeting. Ten days later, a memorial service was held for Phil. Over two thousand family members, friends, and clients gathered to say farewell.

CHAPTER 32
The Key to Bobbie's Heart
2000s

BY THE YEAR 2000, Barb was managing a staff that was now approaching fifty employees, while I was overseeing a staff of ten veterinarians. The clinic was maxed out on space. Once again, we were as crowded as in our early days in the 680-square-foot clinic. Then another opportunity arose. Friendly's Ice Cream closed most of its restaurants in the Buffalo area. One of them was adjacent to our building, and we purchased the property immediately.

It took a year and a half, but eventually we connected the two buildings that sat only 16 feet apart. We remodeled the Friendly's building into a separate, but attached, cat clinic. We became the only veterinary facility in New York State to offer totally separate dog and cat operations under the same roof. Cats had their own waiting room, their own exam rooms, their own pharmacy, their own surgery, and even their own parking lot. And the timing was perfect. Cats had increased from about 15-20 percent of our patients when I entered practice in 1976 to about 45 percent by the turn of the century. And the clinic continued to grow.

* * *

"Ouch! Doc, look at this X-ray before you go back into the exam room. The cat is in a lot of pain. We could only snap one quick view," Michelle, a licensed veterinary technician explained. "If you want the other view, we'll have to sedate Marley."

175

"No way! That can't be!" I said as I glanced at the X-ray. A large metallic object was clearly lodged in the cat's abdomen. "It looks a lot like a size ten scalpel blade, doesn't it?"

Marley, a one-year-old cat, had been vomiting violently for two days and was in obvious distress.

"That's what I was thinking," responded Michelle. "I talked to Mrs. Johnson. They've had the cat for about four months. Her sister adopted Marley at a shelter down in Florida last winter and brought her home. But Mrs. Johnson's niece turned out to be allergic to cats, so the Johnsons took Marley in. And get this! The cat was spayed at a low-cost spay-neuter clinic down South before she was adopted. Is it possible they left a scalpel blade inside *and* it took months for it to cause a problem?"

"Anything is possible, but it sure seems unlikely," I said with a frown. "How would anyone drop a loose blade that's normally attached to a scalpel handle into the abdomen? Well, whatever it is and however it got there, there's no question we need to go in and try to get it out as soon as possible."

I grabbed a size 10 scalpel blade enclosed in its protective wrapper, and I took it into the exam room along with the X-ray. I told Mrs. Johnson that we couldn't be sure what the object was, but that it needed to be removed. I showed her the blade and how similar it looked to the image on the X-ray, but I told her that only one X-ray view could be deceiving. At the same time, I warned her that a loose blade in the abdomen could have already caused irreversible damage.

"Go ahead," she urged. "Do the surgery, Doc. We can deal whatever that object is later. Our six-year old son, Bobbie, is devastated. Bobbie and Marley are best friends. He was up crying most of the night. I left him with my mother in case you had really bad news."

"I can't be certain if we'll have good news or bad, but we'll get Marley into surgery right away. We'll have an answer in a few hours," I promised. "You better go home and prepare the family for the worst. Hope for the best, though. I'll give you a call."

Two hours later, Marley was on the surgery table with a large incision. As I probed gingerly around inside the abdominal cavity, I located a distended loop of small intestine that obviously contained some type of foreign object.

"Well, whatever this is, the cat swallowed it in the last few days. That rules out a scalpel blade unless the Johnsons have surgical supplies lying around the house," I said as I isolated the affected area of the intestine and prepared to make an incision into the bowel.

"It's thicker than a blade, and some of the intestine is pleated above it," I observed. "It may have some sort of string attached."

Within minutes, I extracted the strange piece of metal, and then I ever so gently pulled the string that was trailing along behind it. I breathed a sigh of relief when the string came out without causing further damage or requiring other incisions.

"Wow, we sure were prepared to blame the low-cost clinic down in Florida, weren't we?" I mused. "What a great example of why two different X-ray views are always best, especially when X-raying an abdomen. Two views would have told us instantly that this was not a scalpel blade."

"I think it's some sort of small key," Michelle said, as she cleaned and rinsed the extracted piece of metal.

"I need to write this case up and send it in to the veterinary journal. There is a monthly *What's Your Diagnosis* article and, of course, the correct answer is never what it appears to be at first glance."

Forty-five minutes later, Marley was headed out of surgery with an excellent chance of a full recovery.

"Hi, Mrs. Johnson, I said via telephone. "I've got great news. Marley's surgery went well, and I'm optimistic that she will be fine. Fortunately, the metal object wasn't a blade and it wasn't floating freely inside the abdomen. It was inside her small intestine. It looks like a small key with a string attached. The string looks like it might be a shoe lace."

"Oh no!" she responded. "That's got to be the key to the little savings bank that my parents gave Bobbie on his birthday a few weeks ago. He's been carrying that bank and the key everywhere, opening and closing it all the time. I didn't notice it missing."

Two days later, Marley was ready to head home, but Michelle told me that little Bobbie was still upset. He was sure that it was his fault that Marley had almost died. I told Michelle to ask Mrs. Johnson to bring Bobbie along when she came to pick up Marley so that I could talk to him.

When Mrs. Johnson and Bobbie arrived that afternoon, I made a point to talk to Bobbie first.

"Hi, Bobbie! Marley is doing much better. How are you doing?" I asked as we sat in the exam room waiting for Michelle to bring Marley into the room.

"I ... I ... I want to pay," said the blond-haired boy in a whisper. His head hung low as he plunked the small toy bank on the exam table.

"Bobbie, that's very nice, but I think your mom already paid the bill," I said, winking at Mrs. Johnson behind him. "I want you to know that this was not your fault. Cats love to play with anything long and thin like string, and they sometimes get into trouble when they do. A couple of months ago, I had to remove some sewing thread with a needle still attached that a cat had taken from a lady's sewing machine table. And every year around the holidays, we treat cats that get very sick after playing with tinsel from Christmas trees. Sometimes those cats need surgery as well. I even removed a gold necklace from a cat one time. There's an old saying that 'curiosity killed the cat.' Well, this is a good example of how that can happen. But, fortunately, we were able to prevent Marley's curiosity from doing her in. So in the long run, this was Marley's fault, not yours."

I reached into my pocket and pulled out a few small coins and deposited them into Bobbie's bank.

"But you can help make sure that Marley doesn't get into trouble again with this key and the string," I continued. "Save your money for now and don't open the bank until it's full. I'd like to give the key to your Mom so that she can keep it in a safe place. Then we won't have to worry about Marley playing with it again. OK? Do we have a deal?"

"OK, Doctor. Thank you," Bobbie managed to say quietly.

I thought I saw the smallest smile attempting to show up on Bobbie's sad little face even though his eyes were still moist with tears. Just as that happened, Michelle walked through the door with Marley and placed her gently on the exam room table next to Bobbie's bank. Marley reached over the end of the table and licked Bobbie on the chin, and that tiny smile turned into a huge grin. He giggled and tickled his cat. Bobbie's eyes glistened and gleamed with happiness once again. The little boy rubbed his face on Marley's side to wipe away the tears.

Marley's tongue was far more effective in cheering up Bobbie than my words ever could have been. Although Marley no longer possessed the key to his bank, she clearly still possessed the key to Bobbie's heart.

Yesterday and Today

By 2005 the Brighton-Eggert Animal Clinic had grown to where it was treating over 15,000 pets each year and was employing a staff of over fifty people. Another new development in veterinary medicine was emerging around the country. New corporations were acquiring many larger and more profitable animal hospitals. The rapidly growing amount of student debt carried by new graduate veterinarians was making it more and more difficult for large practices to be sold from one veterinarian to another. In addition, many veterinarians wanted to concentrate on practicing medicine rather than managing a business. Corporations owning large groups of veterinary facilities around the country created an economy of scale that allowed for more efficient operation. National Veterinary Associates acquired the Brighton-Eggert Animal Clinic in June of 2005. I have remained on the staff part-time as a managing veterinarian and consultant since that time.

* * *

As we each look back over our personal journey through time, most people can identify important chapters in their lives. Certainly, the success of the Brighton-Eggert Animal Clinic was the most visible chapter in my life, and many have been familiar with that story. However, I have always considered the years from high school graduation until the opening of the Brighton-Eggert Animal Clinic as the most important chapter, and no one other than Barbara really knew that story. Therefore this book focused primarily on the decade in our lives that set up the success that was to follow. There has never been a doubt in my mind when that journey started. It started when I spotted a cute, red-haired young lady at the lunch counter in a department store shortly after graduating from high school. And together she and I have shared a journey neither of us could ever have imagined.

While the opportunity to use my veterinary talents in a zoo or with wildlife in other areas never presented itself, the success of the business allowed us to refocus energy in that area of our lives at a different level than we ever could have imagined had I not chosen a change in career paths. Barb and I discovered opportunities to travel with veterinary groups to view wildlife in their natural habitats around the world. We visited locations such as Africa, the Galapagos Islands, and Australia. In no time at all, our interest morphed into a passion. We soon found ourselves traveling on our own to more unusual destinations, observing polar bears in northern Canada, Kodiak brown bears in Alaska, and penguins in Antarctica. And those adventures continue.

As for fishing, the other lifelong passion linked with my love of the outdoors, I have had the unique opportunity to travel to many world-class fishing destinations and have had the great privilege to take my father along on most of those trips. And, God willing, those adventures will continue.

None of this would have been possible without the unique things that happened between the summer of 1969 and the summer of 1979, which to me will always represent "The Making of a Veterinarian" chapter of my life.

Along with the people featured in these stories who helped to propel my career forward, there was another more nebulous but nonetheless significant force that aided my path to success. The pets and the pet owners of America and many other parts of the world provided that force.

During the 1970s, it was still acceptable for many owners to allow their dogs to roam freely around their neighborhoods. And other dogs, though confined, often escaped for periods of time while their owners searched the neighborhood calling their names. Both of those groups of dogs were typically fed copious amounts of table scraps poured over basic dry dog kibble. In those days, it was not unusual for veterinary facilities to treat several pets each week that had been hit by cars even in the relatively small clinics where I cultivated my skills. It was fitting, and perhaps almost eerie, that the opening chapter in this book involved a dog that sadly lost her life after being struck by an automobile.

Now fast-forward to those same suburban neighborhoods of today. The shaggy, free-roaming pets are all but gone. They have been replaced by well-groomed, well-behaved dogs being walked by pet owners, in many cases sporting designer leashes attached to designer collars. Many of the dogs have been enrolled in obedience training as puppies. Most of them are fed premium or even holistic diets that were barely in existence three decades ago. Even though our clinic today is radically larger than the settings I practiced in thirty years ago, it is now rare to treat a pet injured by an automobile.

As pets became more important in our lives, the sense of responsibility as a pet owner increased hand in hand with their increased importance. Three decades ago, no one could have envisioned owners walking dogs politely on leashes, carrying plastic bags to collect the bowel movements from their pets. And as the human-animal bond that accompanied this change grew, the human-veterinarian bond grew as well. In short, as pets became more important in our lives, pets' vets became more important as well.

When the stock market is booming on Wall Street, the majority of stocks are increasing in value. Economists and stockbrokers are fond of saying that "a rising tide lifts all boats." I believe the veterinary profession as a whole has reaped a similar benefit. As the human-animal bond exploded, veterinary medicine expanded, too. Everything goes hand in hand, and I was fortunate to become a veterinarian at a time when the profession was evolving to become one of the most respected professions in the nation.

Undoubtedly, we have all observed situations where individual pets seem to have become too important in people's lives. I can assure you that there have been moments when veterinarians also have become too important in the eyes of some pet owners. At times, we too are treated as though we can do no wrong.

As a brief example, many years ago I was examining a dog belonging to the mother of very good friend. As I examined the dog, the owner and I chatted nonstop about her grandchildren and about other mutual friends.

The dog checked out well, and both owner and dog were soon on their way home. Fifteen minutes later, however, I fielded a telephone call from the pet owner. She wanted me to know that the dog had been restless on the car ride home and would not sit down. After the dog got out of the car, it ran in a tight circle several times and moved its bowels. In the bowel movement was the thermometer that I had forgotten to remove. Naturally, I was stunned and embarrassed, yet the client went on and on apologizing for distracting me with her conversations. She was calling because of the broken thermometer and wanted to mail a check to the clinic to cover the loss. I assured her that compensation was unnecessary. I believe a scenario like that could only occur in veterinary medicine.

Pets indeed have come a long way in our lives. The pets are better served and their owners are better rewarded by the closer and closer relationship we all share.

If a person had the opportunity to start life anew, and could choose how he or she might want to return, it would not be a bad choice to decide to return as a pet.

Or perhaps better yet, one might opt to return as its vet.

ACKNOWLEDGMENTS

Rather than naming individual persons, I would like to acknowledge all of the pets seen over the years, all of the clients who presented them for treatment, and all of the employees who assisted as we worked on those furry family members. Together they provided these memorable stories that truly wrote themselves.

This writing began as a fun semiretirement project intended for friends, family, and a few select clients. Thoughts of publication did not surface until many early test readers encouraged me to do so. I received feedback, praise, and editing suggestions from over fifty test readers. The list of helpful persons would be too long to recognize individually on this page. To each and every one of those early readers, I was humbled by your feedback and appreciated your input.

A dozen years ago, I wrote a few short stories that today have evolved into chapters in this book. At about that time, a very special client, now deceased, told me that I failed to fully comprehend the positive effect I had on people's lives via their pets. She urged me to continue writing, but life was too busy. After her passing, her daughter patiently but persistently encouraged me, year after year, to connect the dots and turn those stories into a book. Eventually the seed they planted managed to germinate. For that I will be forever grateful.

And in the end, the feedback from many readers has allowed me to fully comprehend the effects a veterinarian can have on people's lives. And, hopefully, the stories contained herein will return that favor. They will help pet owners better understand the positive effects animals have on their individual lives.

Supporting Pet
and Veterinary Related Causes

From the inception of the decision to publish this book, the goal has been to share a large percentage of the proceeds from sales with multiple animal-oriented organizations. The author wishes to support four core organizations relevant in his life with the sale of each book. In addition, Web sales of the book are structured in such as way as to be available as a fund-raiser for any animal-related, not-for-profit group (for details, please visit **www.pjfpub.com**). The author will not realize any profit from this book unless it proceeds beyond its first printing. However, the core charities will receive support from each and every copy sold from day one. The core groups are described below.

Cornell University College of Veterinary Medicine

Cornell University has offered education in veterinary medicine almost since its inception. Cornell established a formal College of Veterinary Medicine in 1894. All of the colleges of veterinary medicine in North America, including Cornell, serve not only as educators of the veterinarians of tomorrow, but also as leading research institutes for animal-related health problems. Cornell has always been at or near the top of most lists ranking veterinary colleges in North America. Given the importance of Cornell in the author's journey, it is the logical lead institution to receive support from this book.

Readers who might care to learn more about this historic institute or who wish to contribute more support are encouraged to visit Cornell's website (**www.vet.cornell.edu**).

SPCA Serving Erie County

From the author's earliest days in practice in 1976, he has watched the SPCA Serving Erie County grow and evolve for the better. For over thirty years as a member of the Niagara Frontier Veterinary Medical Society (NFVMS), the author has provided courtesy initial health exams for any pets adopted from this institution.

Like all progressive humane societies, the focus of the SPCA's efforts slowly shifted more and more toward insuring that as many adopted dogs and cats as possible be spayed or neutered. In the long run, increasing compliance for pet sterilization is the only practical road to controlling pet overpopulation problems. Initially, the SPCA issued vouchers to new pet owners, allowing them to be neutered at any NFVMS member hospital. This process helped, but unfortunately, even with vouchers for free surgery, many owners never followed through. Eventually, adopted pets were delivered to NFVMS member hospitals for surgery one day prior to their release to the new owners. This step helped even more, but the volume of pets requiring neutering often overwhelmed member hospitals. Soon, it was more practical and more efficient for the SPCA to build an in-house surgery suite, staffed by NFVMS volunteers on a rotating basis. Dr. Philip Weber, cofounder of the Brighton-Eggert Animal Clinic, was the volunteer surgeon on the first official day that surgery was preformed at the SPCA Serving Erie County. Staffing the SPCA surgery with NFVMS volunteers works very well both for the SPCA and the community at large. However, in time, the day arrived when it made more sense for the SPCA to hire in-house staff veterinarians to allow the program to evolve to the next level.

In the long run, the SPCA Serving Erie County has done a wonderful job in addressing the pet overpopulation problem despite the fact that it is serving a region that has been economically stressed for decades. The issue of dog overpopulation has effectively been solved. Finding ways to have similar success in the cat world has proved more challenging, but the situation is slowly improving, and the SPCA Serving Erie County acts as a focal point for addressing that problem.

Readers who might care to learn more about this institution or who wish to contribute more support are encouraged to visit its Web site (**www.yourspca.org**).

Medaille College Veterinary Technician Program

When the author entered practice in 1976, the concept of veterinary technicians was beginning to take shape. Only a handful of colleges around the country were offering the first formal training. A few years later, New York State became one of the first states to license veterinary technicians and to require veterinary practices to utilize properly trained and licensed persons in this important role. Veterinarians have never had to struggle with a lack of potential employees who wish to work with animals. However, finding an adequate supply of properly educated and licensed personnel is often an ongoing struggle in many regions of the country.

Fortunately for veterinary practices in the Buffalo area, Medaille College initiated a veterinary technician program in 1986 that has grown in size and stature every year since that date. The Brighton-Eggert Animal Clinic has had a history of working closely with Medaille College since the inception of this program. Student interns from Medaille have been welcomed in the practice year after year. Furthermore, the clinic established a scholarship in memory of Dr. Philip Weber in 1999. When Medaille College remodeled and expanded its veterinary technician program a few years later, the Brighton-Eggert Animal Clinic donated money to fund the new dog kennel and ward. The author sat on the advisory board for the college's veterinary technician program for many years.

The increased role of veterinary technicians has been instrumental in the evolution of improved medical care for family pets. They fill the role of nurses in the field of human medicine and will no doubt eventually evolve into roles similar to nurse practitioner and physician assistant we all encounter in human medicine today.

Readers who might care to learn more about this institution or who wish to contribute more support are encouraged to visit Medaille's website (**www.medaille.edu**).

PET EMERGENCY FUND

The Pet Emergency Fund (PEF) was established by the Niagara Frontier Veterinary Medical Society (NFVMS) in 1999. The PEF distributes donated funds to member hospitals for one-time intervention in a life-threatening situation for an otherwise healthy pet. Virtually all veterinary hospitals in the Western New York area are members of the NFVMS and participate in the PEF. Funds come from donation boxes in member hospitals and fund-raisers run by employees of all animal hospitals. Recently an annual Run for Rover event has been established in support of this cause.

The Brighton-Eggert Animal Clinic has a long history of supporting and working with the Pet Emergency Fund. We have experienced many situations where owners were able to choose treatment over euthanasia in life-threatening situations because PEF funds were able to cover small portions of the expense involved.

Readers who might care to learn more about this program or who wish to contribute more support are encouraged to visit the Pet Emergency Fund's Web site (**www.petemergencyfund.org**).

Made in the USA
Middletown, DE
03 April 2017